Praise for *Wonderful Marriage*

"*Wonderful Marriage* acknowledges the practical ways to achieve a happy relationship—without compromise or conflict."

—JOHN GRAY, PH.D.,
author of *Men Are from Mars, Women Are from Venus*

"*Wonderful Marriage* isn't just another relationship advice book. It is an honest and authentic approach to making a relationship work. It offers useful guidance and insight into what actually makes a partnership go the distance. Identifying the most vital issues in a relationship—money, sex, and children—is crucial. In addition, the authors don't neglect to address what causes most relationships to fail."

—CHÉRIE CARTER-SCOTT, PH.D.,
author of *If Love is a Game, These are the Rules* and *Negaholics: How to Overcome Negativity and Turn Your Life Around*

"You can tell from the first page the Leeds know what they are talking about. This book is about setting—and getting high standards in marriage. How refreshing! A powerful, practical book written by people who have walked the walk! The Leeds set a high standard for marriage and do convince the reader we all can achieve this. Inspiring; hopeful; touching; informing. I really liked the book and was touched by its authenticity and especially liked the "don't settle" message as well as agreeing on the Big Six! All very doable and durable!"

—PAT LOVE, ED.D.,
co-author of *How to Improve Your Marriage without Talking about It*

"Now you can take out a marriage life insurance plan by simply reading *Wonderful Marriage: A Guide to Building a Great Relationship That Will Last a Lifetime* by Lilo and Gerard Leeds! In it they offer the specific ingredients to connect in all the ways that will create a happy, healthy, and vibrant marriage for life. It's a must-read for all married couples!"

—DR. JANE GREER,
marriage & family therapist, author of *How Could You Do This To Me? Learning To Trust After Betrayal*, www.drjanegreer.com

"Familiarity can breed contempt or contentment. Heed the principles in *Wonderful Marriage* to make sure your relationship stays fresh, sexy, and strong."

—IAN KERNER,
sex therapist and *New York Times* bestselling author

"*Wonderful Marriage* is a wonderful guide to help find true love and enter a relationship that can lead to a great marriage! The chapter about 'Dating with Purpose' is advice I give my clients. Be prepared to devote time and positive energy to finding your partner. Smart dating takes commitment and focus and the results will pay off. Keeping this book by your bedside can help guide you from dating through sharing a whole wonderful life together."

—LISA RONIS,
NYC matchmaker and dating coach

Wonderful
M A R R I A G E

*A Guide to Building a Great Relationship
That Will Last a Lifetime*

LILO & GERARD LEEDS

WITH BESTSLLLING AUTHOR
Terrence Real
Founder of the Relational Life Institute

AND Susan Seliger

BENBELLA BOOKS, INC.
Dallas, Texas

BenBella Books, Inc.
6440 N. Central Expressway, Suite 503
Dallas, TX 75206
www.benbellabooks.com
Send feedback to feedback@benbellabooks.com

Printed in the United States of America
10 9 8 7 6 5 4 3 2 1

Library of Congress Cataloging-in-Publication Data is available for this title.

ISBN 193377139-9

Proofreading by Jennifer Canzoneri and Stacia Seaman
Cover design by Laura Watkins
Text design and composition by John Reinhardt Book Design
Printed by Bang Printing

Distributed by Independent Publishers Group
To order call (800) 888-4741
www.ipgbook.com

For special sales contact Jennifer Canzoneri at jennifer@benbellabooks.com

To our children and their families who add so much to our wonderful marriage

Contents

Acknowledgments

OUR FIRST THANKS GO TO SUSAN SELIGER, our cowriter, for her patience, sense of humor, and writing talent—without her the book would never have gotten done. We want to thank our children and their spouses, Michael, Richard, Daniel, Gregory, Jennifer, Andrea, Anne, Sunita, and Maria, who had wonderful suggestions on the essentials for great marriages and who encouraged us to keep writing when there were a million pressures to do other important things. Our daughter Jen's own questions about marriage helped inspire us to write this book.

Special thanks to all the couples who were interviewed for this book, who spent hours and hours sharing with us the intimate details of their personal lives and marriages. Their stories make an invaluable addition to the book. And further thanks to our longtime personal friends, who also shared their wisdom from their own long and happy marriages. We have changed the names of all interviewees to protect their privacy.

We are also deeply grateful to the more than sixty people who read and reviewed the book in early drafts. Their enthusiastic support kept us going by telling us how the book helped them personally to make positive changes in their relationships and marriages.

To Janet Goldstein, who brought her wide publishing experience to the project, thanks for her commitment, insight, and organizing talent. Much gratitude to Marilyn Allen, our agent, for her hard work, perseverance, and advice. Thanks to Joyce Litner, our executive assistant, who contributed immeasurably by reading and offering advice and helpful comments, keeping things organized, and being wonderfully cooperative at all hours of the day. Appreciation also to Naomi Davis, Lilo's executive assistant, for her help.

Acknowledgments

Thanks to the wonderful people at BenBella Books, Glenn Yeffeth, Jennifer Canzoneri, and Yara Abuata, for their time, creativity, and patience in helping to make this book a success.

Thanks to all the others who helped us along the way with their insights and editorial suggestions. Though we cannot mention you all (you know who you are) you should be proud to know that your contributions will help thousands of couples find love and happiness for a lifetime.

Finally, we are both grateful to each other because writing this book has made our own marriage even better as we tried to live up to our own advice.

—Lilo and Gerry Leeds

Foreword

I T'S NOT DIFFICULT TO IMAGINE that somewhere in your travels you have encountered a couple resembling them—at a gathering of some kind, an alumni weekend, for example, or a fundraiser. You might have met them at someone's Thanksgiving table; they were your hosts' relatives, or their friends. The force of their presence felt at least as much like two lions as two lovebirds. The dance in their eyes when they looked at each other. The way they listened and challenged and *enjoyed* each other

As you watched them, you realized, with a bit of a jolt, that, after thirty, forty, however many years together, these people were completely *into* each other! Far from being a peaceful, boring old pair, you found them stimulating, in fact, exhilarating. And you understood that they were exciting to be with precisely because of the way they excited one another.

In their sixties, seventies, eighties, the only word to describe what they had with each other was *chemistry*. And then—of course, really, how could you not?—you asked yourself the inevitable question: *How have they done it? How have they managed to keep their spark alive after so many years?* And you found yourself seized with a desire to sit down somewhere with a drink or two and quietly, relentlessly, *grill* them: "What about money, in-laws, the kids? How do you handle the little things she does that drive you bonkers when she's been doing them, now, for forty-odd years?" You want to investigate, probe, comprehend. You're dying for them to let you in on the secret—the secret of their wonderful marriage.

Well, if you haven't already, wouldn't it just be terrific to meet such a tried and tested passionate pair? Wouldn't you have a dozen questions?

Let's imagine that you are, right now, in the midst of such an encounter. The couple has agreeably allowed you to corner them for a few hours and you don't hold back; you pepper them with questions, drive the discussion into deep territory. And you are not disappointed. Their answers are hardly the sweet, general platitudes you might have expected, about touching your partner, sleeping in the right bed, and the importance of sex.

Were you ever to find yourself sitting with such a dignified, grandparent-ly, perhaps even great-grandparent-ly pair saying such simple, wise, and thoroughly unexpected things, you would no doubt be thinking something like: "Who in the world *are* these people?" And it would be at just this moment—in my imaginary scene—that someone drifting by, someone who knew the pair well, someone who recognized that particular mixture of curiosity and confusion playing across your features, might take pity on you and join in. "Not your average grandparent types," the passerby would observe. And you might manage to stammer out a reply. "No. Not hardly."

And with your words a thought might follow. "Is this couple extraordinary?" you'd think. "Well, yes. But, then again, that only fits. We haven't spent these last hours talking about a merely ordinary marriage. We've been talking about something so much greater than that." And if by chance, I happened to be the passerby who'd joined you, and if you'd uttered that thought to me, I would have heartily agreed. "Absolutely," I would tell you. "You've been talking about something so much greater than the ordinary that it barely fits in the confines of marriage itself as we most often think of it. What you have been discussing," I would say, "is nothing less than a lifelong romance."

The couple inspiring my flight of fancy is, of course, Lilo and Gerry Leeds, a pair no one in his right mind would call ordinary. Together they founded a high-tech company and grew it to become a half-billion-dollar enterprise. They are well-known and highly respected philanthropists. Between them, they've been awarded seven honorary doctorates. And along the way, they managed to love and be loved by five children and thirteen grandchildren. Ordinary? Not hardly. And yet, the phrase that keeps coming to mind as one reads their book is "down to earth." As accomplished as they are, the Leeds are even more unpretentious. Always willing to laugh at themselves, they told me that they first thought of writing this book precisely because at various functions and parties they'd spent so many hours pinned in corners agreeably answering earnest questions about the secret of their long sustained happiness that one day they joked about writing something down and just handing it to people.

Over time, with much discussion, that jest turned into a serious intent and the Leeds went about it in their typically systematic way. After surveying most of the literature on relationships, particularly studies of unusually happy relationships, a series of rigorous, in-depth interviews were conducted. The insights they share from their own relationship are augmented by expert data and opinion, and illustrated throughout by the real voices of the many men and women who were surveyed. As they neared a finished manuscript, they asked me to join their team. They asked if I would be willing to contribute my insights from my perspective as a couples therapist. Their invitation brought to my mind DVDs that allow you to watch a film and listen in to the director or to an actor's thoughts and observations.

I should confess at this point that when our two sons were little, playing "Cowboys and Indians" was one of many favored pastimes, and somewhere along the way we bestowed upon one another imaginary Native American names. Alexander, the youngest, was "Little Mouse." Older brother Justin was "Running Deer." My wife Belinda was "Wolf Mother," and the name my family saw fit to give me was . . . "Running Commentary." I share this by way of saying that the Leeds's invitation seemed right up my alley.

A word about who I am. The Leeds approached me because of my expertise in relationships. In 1997 my book *I Don't Want To Talk About It: Overcoming The Secret Legacy of Male Depression* was published. It was the first book ever to address the issue of male depression, which at the time was seen as principally a woman's disease in much the same way that alcoholism was seen as a man's disease fifty years ago. I am proud to have played a part in bringing to light a condition affecting millions of men and their families. The book struck a nerve and I began getting calls from around the country, sometimes from men though most often from women. The callers would say that they had tried therapy many times but nothing had worked; they were at their wit's end and a step away from divorce. Could I recommend someone in their area who did the work illustrated in the book? Today, I might well be able to direct them to someone I've trained, but back then I couldn't. At first I referred them to whomever I could but eventually it dawned on me to offer them the possibility of flying to Boston to see if we could turn things around. What quickly evolved was a two-day *relationship intensive* in which our contract coming into the session was that at the end of our time together the three of us would agree that the marriage was either back on track or facing imminent divorce.

In these intensives I found myself using techniques that differed radically from conventional marriage counseling and the results were remarkable. Eighty-five to ninety percent of the marriages were restored and, in follow up, almost all of the couples who followed through with treatment recommendations continued to thrive for years afterward. The media learned of my work and began featuring it. I started teaching this new approach, called *relationship empowerment therapy*, to helping professionals around the country. I founded an institute whose mission, along with professional training, was to reach as many people as possible from all walks of life in order to teach them how to make relationships work, how to develop deep, fulfilling connections to the people around them—in their marriages, in their parenting, and in the workplace. Around the same time I published two books on marriage, most recently, *The New Rules of Marriage*, which I very much see as a companion book to this one.

Now that I've shared the back-story of how the Leeds came to me, I'd like to speak about why I chose them. As an established relationship expert, all manner of projects and proposals cross my desk. Many of them are interesting, many are worthy, and a few are downright compelling. But, to be honest, while I often wish them well, I rarely say "yes" to any of them. I have my own work to do. When I promised to look over the manuscript of *Wonderful Marriage*—even though I'd heard the book was excellent—I still half-expected it to be little more than the memoir of two sweet people with perhaps a noteworthy thought here and there. What I found made me sit up and take notice.

First of all, the Leeds did their homework. What they chose to cull from the literature and research on marriage seemed spot on, and the voices of the men and women in the book added a trenchant, often moving, dimension. But lots of books are well done.

What really got my attention wasn't how they said what they said, but what it was they were saying. *Wonderful Marriage* is no bromide and the Leeds aren't quaint. They're nothing if not no-nonsense businesspeople. But they are, in their way, old-fashioned. Over and over again I found them speaking out for, and giving concrete instructions on how to be... civilized. Now, when I think of a couple that's been married fifty-plus years talking about being kind to each other, my eyes tend to glass over and I tend to stop listening. My assumption is that what they call *kind* I'd call *denial*. But it becomes clear very quickly that this book isn't advice on how to have a pleasant marriage. These authors know about tears and sweat and anger. They know how messy things can get, how hurt you can feel, how distant, resentful, bitter. *But they never lose the thread.*

In the marriage they describe, the one they want you to have, as raw or overwhelmed as you may feel at times, you never forget who you're talking to, nor do you lose sight of why you are talking. You are speaking—they insist we remember—to someone you love. And your purpose in speaking is to share, to cherish, or to make things better. Everything else is little more than a waste of your time. In *relationship empowerment work*, we call this *remembering love*—keeping your eyes on the prize. In a similar vein, implicit in virtually every page of *Wonderful Marriage* is a principle I call *full-respect living*. Full-respect living means making a rock-solid commitment down to the marrow of your bones that, short of outright self-defense, there is no excuse to drop below the line of respectful behaviors. You may not always feel warm and fuzzy toward your partner, there are moments when neither of you feels much love, that's a normal part of marriage. But, no matter how provocative your partner's behavior, no matter how hurt and angry you feel, you will not give in to the impulse to treat him or her with disrespect. Similarly, you don't allow yourself to be on the receiving end of poor treatment and do nothing about it. You may not be able to control the other person, but you needn't just sit there and take it. And while we're focused on self-respect, I want to underline a message central to the Leeds's work that I too feel passionate about: *Don't compromise!*

If you want to compromise on something, compromise on the car you drive, the suit you wear, even compromise on your friends if you have to. But for goodness sake, why in the world would you compromise on the single most important relationship of your life, the person you raise your kids with, face all of life's pleasures and pains with, the one with whom you will grow old and die? The Leeds write: "Too many experts encourage people to be 'realistic.' Our response is: Don't settle. Conventional wisdom says that you can't have everything that you want. That's true! But you can have a great marriage."

I couldn't agree more. Can your relationship be perfect? Of course not. Marriages are made up of two imperfect people. In fact, it is our endearing, maddening, unique characteristics, the quirks of our humanity, that mark us and make us who we are. And it is precisely the collision of your imperfection with mine—and how we *deal* with that collision—that is the stuff, the guts, of intimacy itself. But saying that you can't have everything is not the same as saying that you can't have more than you ever dreamed of. The trick is to know how.

Most people want the dream, the Leeds write, but they don't really know what a great marriage even looks like. Is there a course on how to have a great marriage in college? Do you learn it as a child along with reading and arithmetic? They cite Anne Tyler's observation that we teach our kids more about how to drive a car than how to manage their relationships. I've said to audiences around the U.S. that I want to see basic relationship skills taught starting in pre-school, in elementary school, middle and high school, and in college. I'd like at least as much education to go into a marriage license as a driver's license. How dare we bemoan our appalling divorce rates without doing one thing to prepare people better?

But the Leeds are clear. While it's important to help you avoid becoming another divorce statistic, they are really after bigger game. A "good enough" marriage is in no way, shape, or form good enough for them. And they don't think it should be good enough for you either. Great marriages are possible, they write, only if you set a high standard for both yourself and your partner. In *The New Rules of Marriage*, I wrote: "You don't *have* a great marriage. You *build* one—brick by brick, and skill by skill. We have raised the bar on what we've come to expect in long-term relationships. We have a wonderful new vision. But, so far, we have lacked the means to translate our dreams into our everyday lives."

Until such skills are taught to kids of all ages, we must rely on hard-won wisdom, the insights of researchers and clinicians, to be sure. But also knowledge gained on the front lines, through years of experience. Encountering this manuscript felt to me rather like stumbling upon an undiscovered gem stashed in someone's home, or a dog-eared guide that had been passed from hand to hand. To read it is essentially to allow yourself to be mentored, like learning to fish from someone who has cast out his lure for decades in just about the spot you're standing in. It's the inside scoop, the tricks of the trade. Despite its obvious sophistication, *Wonderful Marriage* still boils down to two old hands telling you what they've learned about how it gets done.

What could be better?

Ten Elements
of a Great Marriage

Happy marriages begin when we marry the ones we love, and
they blossom when we love the ones we marry.

—TOM MULLEN, author of *A Very Good Marriage*

THIS IS NOT A BOOK ABOUT CATCHING a husband, finding a wife, or staying together for the sake of the children.
This book is dedicated to helping you and your partner have
a wonderful life together.

Wonderful Marriage is about setting high standards for whom you
marry. It's about being a great person yourself. It's about giving each
other what you want and need, sharing the problems and the prob-
lem-solving, the work and the play, the laughter and the tears—and
still making a great life for yourselves.

To have such a relationship takes a lot more than luck. Whether
this is your first marriage, your second, or even third, we believe you
have to get the fundamentals right. You have to be willing to work
on your own character. You need to make a real effort to find the
partner who's right for you. You need to love and respect each oth
er, share each other's interests, values, and passions, and allow yourselves room to grow and develop, each in your own way.

It is not enough to be committed to each other, or committed to
being faithful. The real commitment is to do what's best for the other
and share responsibility for a wonderful life together.

If you try to be a good person, find a good partner, and work on your relationship together every day for the rest of your lives, then you can have a wonderful life together—till death do you part.

That's not easy. There is some research that indicates that only 7 percent of all marriages can be considered great marriages. This book is about having one of those, and not settling for second best.

This is not a book for people who think you can achieve great goals without great effort. It is a book for people who believe, as we do, that marriage is a lifelong courtship. If you try to be a good person, find a good partner, and work on your relationship together every day for the rest of your lives, then you can have a wonderful life together—*till death do you part.*

A Great Marriage Is a Lifelong Courtship

We've had a great marriage for more than fifty years. Sharing our love, passions, terrific children and grandchildren, family, and friends has made our lives wonderful and has given both of us a sense of purpose, warmth, and joy every day. We have skied down slopes and climbed up mountains together. We have gone out in the world working together, gone back to school together, and built a business together that was based on many of the same values we brought to our marriage. Many nights we have stayed at home, snuggled up, quietly read books, and talked over politics and ideas. Now we contribute our energy to improve the lives of young people, and both of us continue to deal with the challenges and occasional disagreements of a long life together. We wouldn't trade our marriage for anything in the world.

Almost every young couple we know has noticed how happy we are together and has asked us, "How do you guys do it? How do you stay so close for so many years—and continue to be so compatible and so in love?" One of these young couples even picked our wedding date for their own because they thought it would be lucky.

The majority of Americans say that their main goal in life is to be "happily married for life." It's the dream we have all been brought up on, from fairy tales where the prince and princess "live happily ever after" to the common marriage vows that commit us to be together "till death do us part."

People want the dream, but most people don't know how to achieve it. They don't know what makes a good marriage work or what it looks like and feels like as you live through it day by day. Some years ago, when Gerry was addressing a class at one of the best high schools in the country on how to have a great marriage, he asked the students, aged sixteen and seventeen, if they knew what kind of car they would like to be able to drive by the time they were in their twenties and thirties. Every hand shot up. These young men *and* young women all knew exactly what they thought constituted a "great car." They knew the make and model, how much it currently cost, what image it projected, why they wanted to drive it. They had given the matter a great deal of thought and study.

However when he asked those same kids what kind of marriage partner they would want in the next ten or fifteen years, he gazed out on a roomful of blank stares. They did not have a clue about what was involved in a "great marriage." Some said their parents never really talked to them about what goes into a marriage. Others said the marriages they saw on TV or in the movies weren't very realistic or appealing. Still others said they weren't sure they ever wanted to get married because they had never seen a marriage worth having and so many people they knew were divorced.

These high school students are not all that different from everybody else we have talked to on this subject. Whether you are single, married, or near a commitment, you may have only a vague idea of what a really good relationship or marriage is. Like almost half the population, you may have grown up with divorce and, perhaps, fear you'll repeat the pattern. Or, just as likely, you may see many marriages around you that are not great models to follow. If your parents had a good marriage you may take for granted that yours will be equally good.

So, it isn't surprising that many of us don't know what a great marriage is. Schools don't teach it along with reading, writing, and arithmetic, even though picking the right person to marry and building a wonderful life together will be, for most people, the most important and meaningful aspect of living a happy life. Novelist Anne Tyler captured this observation in *Breathing Lessons*:

> "I mean you're given all these lessons for the unimportant things—piano-playing, typing...how to balance equations, which Lord knows you will never have to do in normal life. But how about parenthood? Or marriage, either, come to think of it. Before you can drive a car you need a state-approved course of instruction, but driving a car is nothing, nothing compared to living day in and day out with a husband."

Choosing the right marriage partner has more influence over your lifelong happiness than any other decision you make—more significant than what college you attend, what career path you follow, or how much you earn in life. The head of a very successful technology company once said to us, "I've succeeded in everything in my life except my marriage." None of the other successes he'd achieved could make him as happy as having a good marriage would have.

That's why we wrote this book.

Ordinary People, Extraordinary Marriages: How to Make the Dream Come True

We would like to share with you what we have learned about how to have a great marriage. We firmly believe that a great marriage is possible—even in these stressful, fast-changing, twenty-first-century times. Too many experts, parents, "helpful" friends, and talk-show hosts encourage people to be "realistic." Our response is: Don't settle. Conventional wisdom says that you can't have everything you want. That's true! But you can have a great marriage, if you're willing to get yourself ready and are committed to finding the right person for you. We want to inspire you to meet that person. If you're already in a serious relationship or marriage, we want to help you discover your potential for a great life together and show you the steps to get there.

Too many experts encourage people to be "realistic." Our response is: Don't settle. Conventional wisdom says that you can't have everything you want. That's true! But you can have a great marriage.

We started to analyze what we thought made our marriage work. Then we talked with many of our friends who also had good marriages. We tracked down dozens of happily married couples across the country. These were people who had been together for anywhere from six to sixty years and who rated their marriage "great." We conducted extensive interviews with them to find out their secrets to success.

They had extraordinary marriages, but they were not extraordinary people. They loved talking about their marriages and sharing their high points with us. But they also were not immune to problems, crises, and conflicts. One couple lost a child; one husband became deaf after military combat; a wife contracted MS; several lost jobs. Almost all of them had repetitive fights and their ample share of arguments.

The good marriages endured because both partners were able to put love and respect first; they deal openly and honestly with disagreements, share the work and decision making, have fun together, and are willing to change and grow. The great marriages became even stronger as a result of the partners' living through difficult times together. And most found enormous comfort in their ability to help each other see beyond the pain to the pleasure they could share.

Here are three truths we have learned:

- Great marriages are possible if you both set high standards for yourselves and each other.
- To have a great marriage you have to get off to the right start: be a great partner yourself, marry a great partner who is right for you, and learn what it takes to achieve the essential elements of a great marriage.
- Love, by itself, is not enough—neither is luck. You have to find the right partner and you both have to be committed and will-

ing to work on your marriage every day of your lives to keep making each other happy. Ask yourself, "What have I done today to make my partner's morning just a little nicer, the evening a little more fun?"

If you can learn about what a great marriage is and how to get there, you have a better chance to achieve one. Maya Angelou once wrote: "You did the best that you knew how. Now that you know better, you'll do better." And we want to do more than keep your marriage from turning into a divorce statistic. We want to help you have a marriage that is great *right from the start—and stays that way*. We want your marriage to be happy. We want you to say to yourselves: "This is wonderful—our whole life should be like this forever."

The Practical Advantages of Marriage

Beyond the *emotional* benefits we've discussed, there are also considerable practical benefits. Many of the following points have been researched and documented in *The Case for Marriage: Why Married People Are Happier, Healthier, and Better Off Financially* by Linda J. Waite and Maggie Gallagher.

- **In a good marriage, people have better, more satisfying sex— more often and for more years—than unmarried people.**
  Married men and women not only have sex more often, but they report that they enjoy it more both physically and emotionally than do their unmarried counterparts.
- **Married people live longer, healthier lives than unmarried people.**
  Married men and women live a substantially healthier and longer life, compared to single or divorced men and women. They get sick less; they have fewer diseases; they survive disease better. Being unmarried can cut ten years off a man's life. For a woman, not marrying shortens her life span by more years than if she were married and contracted cancer.
- **Children of married couples enjoy better health, wealth, and happiness than children of unmarried parents.**

THE MARRIAGE ADVANTAGE

If you're on the fence about marriage, wondering whether it is really worth it when staying single or living together seems so much simpler, it wouldn't be surprising. Today, men and women have alternatives to marriage. Unlike the conventions of only a few decades ago, women are not labeled "old maids" if they don't marry young. Nor do they have to depend on marriage for financial security. Men don't need marriage to gain respectability. Neither needs the benefit of a marriage certificate to enjoy sex without stigma. And if they do get married and decide they want out, they can get divorced more easily than ever before. So why marry?

- Can you think of anything more appealing than the idea of waking up next to someone you love—every day of your life?
- What could be more satisfying than living with someone who shares your passions, sexual and otherwise, who keeps you from being lonely—and who also knows when to leave you alone?
- Can you imagine anything better than having a person by your side, all your life, who loves and respects you, supports you, gives you encouragement and security, shares your values and priorities, who helps you make better decisions in life, and enables you to accomplish so much more than you would alone?

Children living with parents who are not married, on average, are not as physically or mentally healthy, as well educated, nor as successful later in life as those living with married couples, asserts a 2003 report by the National Marriage Project entitled, "The State of our Unions: The Social Health of Marriage in America."

- **Marriage boosts financial security.**

Getting married can boost your standard of living by about one-third, and that financial gain improves further over time. Married men earn more than unmarried men, partly because, with a family to support, they are strongly motivated. But they also earn more because they tend to lead more settled lives, making them better employees. Because unmarried couples tend to keep their money separate, their wealth does not increase with the length of the marriage as it does with married couples.

Steps to a Great Marriage:
How This Book Can Help You Get There

What stage of life and love are you in right now? Are you just starting to "date with purpose"—our term for serious dating with a view to marriage? Have you recently broken up or divorced a partner and are about to start dating again? Are you in a serious relationship but unsure if you're ready for marriage? Or have you been married, perhaps for years, and are now wondering whether you can make your relationship even better?

No matter where you find yourself right now, this book can help you achieve the most important goal of your life: an exciting and satisfying relationship that lasts a lifetime. We firmly believe that you can find a love that will grow deeper and stronger, that you can share all the stages of a life together, and that you can discover and build your happiness as you create rituals, raise children, make friends, reach out to your community, and work to make your hopes and dreams come true.

We found ten time-tested elements that great marriages have in common. They are simple but powerful habits of the mind and heart that help us bring out the best in each other. These elements correspond to the ten chapters in this book:

1. GET YOURSELF READY

When you are the kind of person others can count on to be honest and caring, you are likely to attract the kind of partner you will be able to love and trust for a lifetime. When you develop the character traits that you admire in others, you feel good about who you are, you see the good in others, and, equally important, you expect others to see and respect the good in you.

2. DATE WITH PURPOSE

Dating for fun, dating to meet lots of new people, or dating to avoid being alone is not the same as dating with purpose. Dating with the purpose of marriage means getting clear about the qualities you really want in a partner and then seeking out people who have those qualities. There is a kind of ease and acceptance couples feel when they know they are with the right person.

3. PUT LOVE AND RESPECT FIRST

Love and respect build through a series of everyday exchanges, not necessarily grand gestures: speaking kindly to each other, making sure to praise (not criticize) each other every day, showing up for a date on time or calling if you're running late, not saying a word even though you've heard your partner tell that joke three times before. Ask yourself this simple question: "What would make my partner's life a little nicer or better?" If you can put your partner's needs first without sacrificing your own, if you can bring out the best in each other, you will accomplish far more *together* than either of you could alone.

4. AGREE ON THE "BIG SIX"

To be happy, couples don't need to be clones of each other. But they do need to come to an agreement on six critical issues before they decide to marry—children, money, religion, recreation, sex, and acceptable behavior. Many couples set aside their differences over whether or not they want to start a family, their too-frequent and unresolved fights, or their lack of physical passion for each other. The happiest couples know that time and commitment do not resolve these core issues. They have to discuss these issues openly and make sure they agree before going forward.

5. DECIDE ABOUT MARRIAGE

Happy couples make clear commitments to each step of their relationship—from dating exclusively, to living together, to getting engaged and married. Their openness builds trust and respect. When the time is right, they celebrate their growing bonds privately and publicly, which becomes a habit for a lifetime.

6. COMMUNICATE LOVINGLY

If you try each day to be considerate, warm, polite, affectionate, courteous, in short, *nice*, to your partner, you will set the tone for a lasting relationship. Happy partners know that honest communication is central to enjoying each other and getting along every day. All couples have their differences and disagreements, but happy couples are different in this respect: they communicate lovingly, resolve their differences as they arise—and they (almost) never go to bed angry.

7. MAKE SEX GREAT FOR BOTH OF YOU

Sex is more than an event; it is a wonderful way to express and experience your love. Loving couples have a natural attraction for each other, but they also grow and learn from each other. In a wonderful relationship both partners appreciate the importance of sensual pleasure to the relationship, share a desire to satisfy each other, are sensitive to each other's needs, insecurities, and desires, and are attuned to each other's changing sexual rhythms.

8. SHARE THE WORK AND DECISION MAKING

No matter who earns what, you have to share the decisions that affect your lives. However busy or stressed out either of you may feel, both of you have to make *some* contribution to keeping the household running in a way that makes each of you feel appreciated, valued, and happy.

9. ENJOY RAISING CHILDREN

Not all happy couples have children; if it's a mutual decision it is surely the right one. For us, and for most couples, there is nothing that keeps two people closer than the joy and awe-inspiring responsibility of raising children together. Children themselves bring so much love into a family—as well as stretching everyone's capacity to love and respect others.

10. BUILD A HAPPY, HEALTHY LIFE TOGETHER

Being healthy and having fun keep you and your relationship full of energy, joy, and passion. Without shared activities and pleasures, "dates," a circle of loving friends and relatives, and satisfying individual pursuits, a relationship can seem like it's all work and no play. When two partners maintain a playful, optimistic spirit they are well on their way to achieving a happy and satisfying lifetime partnership.

Do Everything with Love: The "Strawberries" Story

We've written this book to be inspirational as well as practical, because believing a great relationship is possible is as important as working to make it so. Remember, you are not just looking for someone you can live with, but someone you can't live without. We hope this book, *Wonderful Marriage*, will make a difference on your way to creating a wonderful, happy life together as partners and lovers.

If we had to simplify what it takes to have a great marriage to one essential element, it would be this: *You both have to do everything with love.* A favorite story of ours captures the idea.

One evening not long ago, Lilo and Gerry were at a dinner party. "I found myself seated beside an attractive young woman in her twenties," Gerry explains. "We were talking about love and marriage. By dessert she said, 'How will I know when I've found the right partner?' Just then someone passed a bowl of strawberries. Looking at the berries, I said, 'The right guy will want to give you the best strawberries. Always. And you'll want to give him the best strawberries, too.'

"A year later she called us, all aglow, and said, 'I think I found somebody who wants to give me the best strawberries.' She married him, had three children, and now has a happy and loving marriage. She says her husband still wants to give her the best strawberries . . . as she does for him."

If we had to simplify what it takes to have a great marriage to one essential element, it would be this: *You both have to do everything with love.*

PART ONE

Looking for Love

CHAPTER ONE

Get Yourself Ready: Your Character Counts

Character may be manifested in the great moments,
but it is made in the small ones.

—PHILLIP BROOKS, nineteenth-century preacher
and lyricist for "O Little Town of Bethlehem"

NO MATTER WHERE YOU STAND IN YOUR love life—whether you are in the early stages of dating, in a serious relationship, or already married—your quest to have love last a lifetime begins with yourself. Every choice you make on a daily basis shapes who you are and who you are becoming. As Aristotle said, "We are what we repeatedly do." The choice to do the right thing may not always be easy, but the results are well worth it. When you develop into the kind of person you are proud to be, you'll have the best chance of attracting the kind of person you will also admire. In other words, you will become the kind of person who will attract the kind of person you'll want to wake up next to and kiss good night for the rest of your life.

The happy couples we interviewed talked about several key character traits they were looking for in a partner. They wanted someone who was honest, kind, emotionally mature, with a positive outlook on life. They also talked about looking for someone attractive, compassionate, patient, and loyal, and many other fine qualities. In short, they were looking for someone who was *nice*.

Every choice you make on a daily basis shapes who you are and who you are becoming.

If you possess those traits, you are far more likely to attract the kind of partner you will be inclined to love, admire, and respect for a lifetime. And you are likely to bring out those qualities in the person you are with. If, on the other hand, you are inclined to be selfish and self-centered, emotionally troubled, or unhappy, you're not likely to attract the kind of person you'll want to marry.

To have a great relationship, you have to start with yourself—ideally *before* you get married, but it is never too late for improvement. Your life—and all your relationships—will change as you develop the traits that define a person of good character. As our son Greg pointed out, "It's not enough to marry the right partner, you need to work to be the right partner."

Aim to Be Attractive and Appealing, in Mind and Body

Strive to become as healthy, physically fit, well-dressed, and well-behaved as you possibly can be. You don't need to strive to be something you are not—we cannot all look like models, nor do we need to. Simply eat right, exercise, get enough sleep, pay attention to hygiene and the way you dress. When you look as good as you can, it shows you care enough about yourself and the people you meet to make the effort to look your best. Looks are only part of the picture. Manners matter, too. Be friendly to everyone you encounter, from the people in the elevator to the grocery store clerks. You can rarely go wrong by demonstrating good manners and respectful, polite conduct. But the reverse behavior—boorish table manners or rudeness—can often put an end to relationships before they start. It's not simply that you are showing that you have "class." More important, you are showing that you are considerate and courteous. Those traits will go far in attracting the kind of person you want.

Work on developing your knowledge. Everybody loves an easygoing conversationalist who is well-informed, well-intentioned, and, better yet, funny. Reading the newspaper and staying current on events will always provide a supply of material to keep the conversation lively and interesting. Remember, you don't have to do all the talking. When you ask questions of others—and listen with genuine interest to the reply—you are also showing how attractive, appealing, and intelligent you really are.

Radiate a Sense of Optimism

You may feel you weren't born an optimist, but research has found that you can cultivate a more positive view of life. Those who see the world with a sense of hope tend to be people others enjoy being around. If you make an effort to look for the good in others, you are more likely to find that others will find the same in you.

One way to deepen your sense of optimism is to "develop a good eye and a good heart," as Esther Jungreis puts it in her book *The Committed Marriage*. Seeing the world with "a good eye" means you are always looking to see the good, not the bad, in others. It doesn't mean you view the world uncritically or hesitate to make proper judgments. But it does mean that you are not looking for what is wrong with the world so much as what is right.

"People who are endowed with loving-kindness and a good eye have something more magnetic than beauty or a handsome face," says Jungreis. "[It's] an inner charm that radiates. Kindness illuminates their faces, and even if, with the passage of time, she becomes flabby and wrinkled and he becomes bald and potbellied…the charm remains, and because of it, they will always find their partners enchanting. And that is the most important ingredient for a good marriage."

"Tom sees the good side of things and that just brings out the best parts in me," says Colleen, who has known Tom for twenty years, since high school. They have been married and living on the West Coast for seven. "I think many of us have a tendency to be self-defeating; we know our own worst qualities. I sure do. But Tom is that one person who makes me feel more confident, more comfortable with who I am. He makes me a better person. That, to me, is the greatest part of this relationship."

Be Caring and Compassionate

Compassion is one of the traits that comes up most often when couples discuss what attracted them and keeps them together years later. Possessing compassion means you are able to care not only for your partner, but also for everyone in your life—family, business associates, teachers, neighbors. You are kind to others and a good listener. You express gratitude for the kindnesses of others. It also means you're willing to spend the time and effort it takes to make someone else's life better.

"I remember when one of our businesses was doing poorly, Gerry and I were both pretty worried about it," recalls Lilo. "But even though we didn't have much money, I'd try to cheer him up by making a nice meal or suggesting we go out somewhere to relax and talk about the situation. And with the children, we thought it was important to talk about other people who were in trouble and ask the kids to think how they would feel if they were in that position. We'd read a column in the *New York Times* called 'Neediest Cases,' and we'd ask each child to pick someone they wanted to help out." Lilo adds with a laugh that "when it came to teaching the children to be compassionate with each other, that was a little harder until they became adults. Now they care about the suffering of others and have a passion to try to change it."

You also have to be willing to accept your partner's caring for you. Some people find that hard. They think it is an admission of weakness. The truth is we all need help sometimes; we cannot take care of ourselves completely alone. At those times, there is nothing one is more thankful for than having a compassionate partner.

Be Honest, Trustworthy, and Reliable

Being honest couldn't be easier to describe: You don't lie, and you don't cheat. When asked, you tell the truth. Even when you're not asked, you tell the truth. If you play by these rules, you have a much greater chance of finding a partner who does the same.

If you master honesty, you're well on your way to being trustworthy and reliable. If you can consistently be depended upon to keep your promises and do what you say you'll do, you'll be a much-valued human being at work, as you date, marry, and ultimately as you build a long life together. Being honest can be difficult, but in the long run it's the right way to live. But you can temper your honesty with discretion, courtesy, and tact.

Being honest couldn't be easier to describe: You don't lie, and you don't cheat. When asked, you tell the truth. Even when you're not asked, you tell the truth.

"I have two daughters in their twenties and this is what I have told them about what to look for in finding the right person: Look for someone who is honest, first and foremost," says Beth, married to Alan for twenty-eight years. "Of course, I also tell them to find someone who loves them and whom they can truly depend on. I tell them it takes commitment, and they have to work at it. Both sides have to be willing to put their spouse ahead of themselves much of the time. Then they'll have a good marriage."

Be Patient, Use Self-Control

It is not always easy to think before you act or speak. But that ability will keep you out of a lot of trouble in life…and in marriage. If you can practice patience in small ways with your partner, co-workers, and the people you encounter every day, you will find it almost second nature to continue behaving with tolerance and decency toward everyone. Getting angry is indulging yourself—and is not fair to your partner.

Exercising patience and self-control is a means to greater self acceptance. It is a trait that will serve you well on the job. And your mate will thank you for it, too.

What Elizabeth respects and admires in her husband, Larry, is his self-control and calm demeanor, no matter what is happening in their lives. "The man I dated before Larry would yell and get angry when things didn't go his way; it was painful. Being with Larry was a huge difference—like a breath of fresh air. He loves me for what I am, not what he wants me to be."

19

Arthur, who has known and loved his wife, Sarah, since he was sixteen and she was seventeen, echoes a similar sentiment.

"One of the things I admire in my wife is her patience, especially in her job as a mother," says Arthur. "There is no way I could do the job she is doing with our daughter—she's phenomenal."

Accept Responsibility

One of the biggest challenges in a relationship is whether you can accept responsibility for your actions—and your inactions. Sometimes the things you don't do ("Oops, I forgot to pick up the tickets") can have as much impact as the things you do. Because we all make mistakes, being able to own up to them, say you're sorry for them, and try to make up for them go a long way toward easing the inevitable tensions that arise in daily life.

Sometimes the things you don't do ("Oops, I forgot to pick up the tickets") can have as much impact as the things you do.

In our society it often seems like a self-centered, get-what-you-can attitude is the only way to make it. Despite the images of success and relationships we see in the media, the opposite is really true. Personal responsibility is a quality that everyone admires, whether they find it in a friend, a coworker, or a lover.

"When we were growing up, my father told me over and over, 'Be honest. It doesn't matter how hard it is. Be honest,'" recalls Gerry. "We were one of the last families to escape Nazi Germany before World War II, and even though time was short, I remember my father going around to everyone he did business with to make sure all his debts were paid and his accounts were settled before we left. He didn't have to do that—people would have understood given the circumstances. But he did. So having a sense of responsibility and good character are very important to me. And I knew from the moment I met Lilo that they were important to her, too."

Interestingly, when we become more responsible ourselves, we raise the standards of how others interact with us. If you arrive on time, follow through on your commitments, and avoid blaming others, the people around you will do the same. If they don't, you will recognize their behavior much more quickly and you will be able to make choices about how you want your relationships with them to develop.

It is also important to recognize that you are accountable for your actions, not only in your personal relationships, but also in your role as a member of the larger community. Helping others allows you to stand out as a person of good character.

Maria and Anthony both agree that their marriage is so successful because they can depend on each other. "If I'm having a problem, Anthony is right there to help me through it," says Maria. "That's the one thing I especially admire about him. He's a good person to everybody. Right now, even when he doesn't feel all that well, he takes care of his aging aunts. He's always available to help everybody, neighbors, too."

Develop Your Individuality

Many people have a vision of a loving relationship as one in which two people are so close that they almost meld into one person with completely shared likes, dislikes, and passions. Psychologist David Schnarch calls this "a fusion fantasy."

In his book *Passionate Marriage* Schnarch argues that the strongest and happiest relationships are those in which the opposite of fusion occurs. These are couples in which each partner is able to establish his or her own unique, independent character. Through a process called *differentiation* each partner is able to become distinct without being distant, an individual without being egocentric or selfish.

"Differentiation involves balancing two basic life forces: the drive for individuality and the drive for togetherness," Schnarch writes. "Giving up your individuality to be together is as defeating in the long run as giving up your relationship to maintain your individuality. Either way, you end up being less of a person with less of a relationship."

As the psychologist Erich Fromm put it, "In love the paradox occurs that two beings become one and yet remain two." From this perspective, developing your character does more than make you a "good catch," it enables you to maintain your unique sense of self, even after you have entered into a serious, loving relationship.

Be Fair, Play Fair

From the earliest age, children seem to have built-in radar for justice. We know immediately when someone is not playing fair—and we don't like it. Parents are often taken aback when their young offspring detail such injustices as who got more hugs, cookies, play dates, or toys for their birthday. As children mature, we try to teach them the difference between "fair" and "the same." We teach them about justice and honor at school and with friends.

When we find people who display a sense of fair play in all that they do—whether it's playing sports or doing their fair share at work or giving unselfishly to their lover—most of us instinctively trust and admire them.

"Not everybody might think the way we share things is fair, but we decided we'd each do what we like to do—and that seems fair to us," says Joyce. "Harry likes to cook so he does most of that, and I do most of the cleaning up. I actually like doing handyman jobs around the house—I did them with my father growing up. Harry doesn't mind that that's usually what the man of the house does. It works for us."

When we find people who display a sense of fair play in all that they do, most of us instinctively trust and admire them.

Demonstrate Loyalty and Commitment

If you practice being faithful and loyal to friends and family, it will seem only natural to continue the pattern with your lover. A steadfast friend and partner is a "value far above rubies." As Thomas Jefferson advised: "In matters of style, swim with the current; in matters of principle, stand like a rock."

"I'll tell you what I admire about Pat: his faithfulness," says Louise about her husband of sixty years. Both have stood by the other, in sickness and in health. A year after they married, he went off to serve in World War II and returned deaf. Twenty years after that, she developed multiple sclerosis and now has to use a wheelchair. "He has been my rock, believe me. He has never given up."

"When she falls down—and she falls down easily—I just lay down with her on the floor," Pat says with a loud laugh. "One time I came into the living room and I saw her lying on the floor. She was kind of crying a little, so I lay down on the floor next to her and I said, 'What are you doing down here?' Of course she started to laugh and I just wiped away the tears. I call her Miss Gutsy. She's got guts enough to do anything. Believe me, there were days when we were working on the business together and she'd wake up hurting so much, I'd tell her, 'Honey, why don't you stay in bed.' But she just said, 'No, help me get dressed because if I lie here I'll only think of myself. I need to get to work.'

"I admire that attitude," Pat says. "I wouldn't change anything about her, even her MS. I wish she could get rid of it. But I love her as she is."

Eliminate Bad Habits: Get Help If You Need It

If you feel you have problems being the person you want to be, talk to a friend, counselor, or psychologist. While we cannot transform ourselves into someone completely different, all of us are able to grow and change, if we are adequately motivated. Sometimes it takes outside help; it is certainly worth the effort.

CHAPTER TWO

Date with Purpose: Find the Person Who's Right for You

Some enchanted evening
You may see a stranger,
You may see a stranger
Across a crowded room
And somehow you know,
You know even then
That somewhere you'll see her again and again.

—RICHARD RODGERS & OSCAR HAMMERSTEIN II,
from "Some Enchanted Evening," South Pacific

MANY OF US DREAM ABOUT FINDING OUR perfect mate simply by gazing across a crowded room and seeing someone who catches our eye and captures our heart. It does happen. Our own first encounter more than five decades ago had some of that quality of love at first sight.

"I noticed Lilo immediately when I walked into the ski lodge in the Adirondacks on New Year's Day," Gerry recalls. "First I saw how pretty she was. I liked the way she talked and smiled. Then I realized she was playing an obscure European game that I had played as a child. I noticed she was sitting there with another guy, but that didn't stop me. I said, 'May I play?' She said, 'Do you know how?' 'Doesn't everybody?' I replied. She was surprised that I knew what it was. I sat down to play the game with her, and she won.

"The next day, when I saw her on the slope skiing with friends and members of her ski club, it was obvious she was a very good skier. I joined them for a run or two and we kidded around. I was very attracted to her. She was more than pretty. She was fun to be with, intelligent, and her background was very similar to mine. I felt an immediate bond. She was different from all the other girls I had dated. Right there on the slope it crossed my mind that she could easily be the woman I would marry someday.

"When I got back to New York it took me six weeks to locate the little ski club she had come with. I joined it immediately. Nine weeks later we were engaged.

"Today, we have five children, thirteen grandchildren, and a happier life than either one of us could have imagined possible back at that ski lodge."

Many couples in great marriages talk about a first flicker of interest that developed into something more. They speak of feeling a special bond or kinship. They relish every trait and detail of personal history they have in common. ("We both love taking long walks." "His favorite book was my favorite, too.") They take pleasure in listing the qualities they admire in the other: intelligence, spunk, sense of humor, honesty, beauty, integrity, creativity, a sense of adventure.

Are You Really Ready for Serious Dating?

It doesn't matter if you just met someone today, if you are already seriously dating, or if it takes you more time to find the right person. The key to a great relationship isn't getting lucky, it's getting serious about who you are and what you want. You have to decide if you are ready to "date with purpose."

- Are you ready for a serious relationship?
- Are you mature and responsible enough to consider getting married?
- Are you clear about the most important qualities you seek in a partner and are you determined to find them?

When you date with purpose, each date can help you figure out what kind of person would make you happy—and what kind of person wouldn't.

The key to a great relationship isn't getting lucky, it's getting serious about who you are and what you want.

"Richard and I were raised the same, so we just understand each other and do things in similar ways," explains Maryanne of her husband of seventeen years. "When we were dating and were invited to a friend's house for dinner. I thought it was important to bring flowers or a gift. That's how I was raised, and he was, too. So when I said I needed to swing by the bakery to pick up a cake to bring, there was no argument. Or when we entertain at our house now, I like to cook the whole dinner thing, make a real effort, not just put out beer nuts or junk food. I think that's really important, and Richard does, too."

If you've been single for a while, you may feel that you've already been through the dating mill. Or you may feel like dating is an ordeal that you'll never master. But once you begin dating with purpose you'll have a new sense of focus and motivation to guide and inspire you.

You'll be surprised at how clarifying where you stand and what you want will reduce your anxiety about dating. You won't take things so personally. You'll see that if someone rejects you, it isn't because you are an unworthy person; it is probably because you weren't right for each other, and it was necessary for you to move on and find someone who is. Such a perspective takes a lot of the pain out of the process and makes it more enjoyable.

When you date with purpose you are learning what kind of person you are really attracted to, who gets your heart beating fast and makes you feel as if you're counting the minutes until you see each other again.

Kathryn and Roger have been married eight years, both for the second time. They knew they wanted something different in their second marriage.

"We both wanted someone kinder and more understanding," says Roger. "It wasn't a physical attraction at first—I know that sounds crazy, because it is now. It was a spiritual attraction. Kathryn and I became sort of soul mates; we understood each other."

Kathryn concurs. "We trusted each other. We enjoyed being together. We made each other laugh. And that was something neither of us had had in a long time."

Knowing what they wanted paid off. "I still get butterflies in my stomach when I'm at work and I think about her."

Finding a lifetime partner is unquestionably exciting, but it is also challenging. Gone are the days when most people encountered their love interest at high school or college. If you are like many others in the United States, you may have moved far away from your hometown and where you went to college. You may not have a network of friends and family to introduce you to new people and to include you in events where you can have fun at the same time you expand your social life. So it probably will not surprise you to hear that men and women are marrying several years later than they used to, up four years to age twenty-seven for men, and up five years to age twenty-five for women since the 1960s.

Meeting people isn't the only hurdle. Consider this: Our expectations for marriage are higher than ever. It makes sense because our standards for everything have risen. We want it all. We want healthier, more exotic foods from all over the globe—in any season. We want bigger houses (the average new house in the United States is about 30 percent larger than fifty years ago), more television stations than anyone a generation or two ago ever dreamed of, and faster, cheaper travel. We want shopping malls with hundreds of stores, not just a handful of local stores.

With marriage, too, we want more than ever before. Financial security and a safe place to raise children are not enough. We want love, passion, and fulfillment, along with the rest. And we want our love to last a lifespan that now stretches a good ten or twenty years longer than it did a century ago. And why not? Why shouldn't we have a great marriage?

We should. But all of these changes in society, plus the intimidating 50 percent divorce rate, make it seem harder to find and choose the right partner with confidence.

Whether you are working toward your first marriage, or your second or third, you need to be aware of the essentials of finding a great partner for life. There are four things you'll need to consider:

1. What do you want in a partner?
2. What strategies will you use to meet a great partner?
3. If this is your second (or third) marriage (or long-term relationship), what are you going to do differently?
4. If you are dating someone casually, when is it time for greater commitment?

1. What Do You Want in a Partner?

Though some people believe opposites attract, research suggests otherwise. The more partners have in common, whether it's comparable backgrounds or similar experiences growing up, the stronger the bond between them will be.

You may not know exactly what you're looking for, but you need to start thinking seriously and realistically about what is important to you. What would make you happy? What could you contribute to a marriage with this partner, and what can you reasonably expect or hope for?

Though some people believe opposites attract, research suggests otherwise. Most long and happy marriages are built on two people being more alike than they are different—they both have in common the traits that are important to each of them. They share many of the same beliefs, values, likes, and dislikes and are also able to grow and learn together. The more partners have in common, whether it's comparable backgrounds or similar experiences growing up, the stronger the bond between them will be.

One starting point is to draw up a list of those traits and characteristics that are most important to you in an ideal mate.

David and Beth met at a wedding, got married two years later, and have been together for thirty-six years.

"We met at my brother's wedding—she was a friend of the bride, and we liked each other right away," recalls David. "She was honest, wholesome, had good values, she came from a good family. She was also pretty. She seemed to have all the characteristics I was looking for in a woman."

RANK THE QUALITIES YOU SEEK IN A MATE

Luck isn't enough when you are searching for the right mate, nor is persistence, though both help. To improve your chances for success it helps to have a good idea of what you are looking for. Below are qualities to consider when trying to describe the kind of person you want to spend the rest of your life with.

Be as specific as possible about your wants and desires, listing several items for each category. You can't be superficial about the list. Jotting down "slender and sexy" or "handsome and rich" just won't suffice. Focus on those qualities that are most important to you and compatible with your personality. Rate each of the traits on a scale of 1 to 4.

1 = Not important
2 = Somewhat important
3 = Very important
4 = Essential, not willing to do without

___ **Age:** Are you looking for someone older, younger, your age? What age range is right for you?

___ **Physical appearance:** Note your preferences, though physical appearance probably will not remain at the top of your list of what's most important.

___ **Personality and style:** What do you regard as an attractive personality? Consider: a sense of humor, manners, ambition, physical demonstrativeness, temperament, energy level.

___ **Sexual attractiveness:** What excites you in a person? What turns you off? Do you want a person who likes to touch and be touched?

___ **Character:** What traits do you value most? Consider: honesty, compassion, kindness, reliability, self-control, leadership, passion, loyalty, generosity, sense of humor.

___ **Recreation and leisure interests:** How would you like to spend your free time with your partner? Consider: travel, sports, reading, music, dancing, walking, camping, cooking, nature, animals, evenings with friends or family.

___ **Communication and comfort level:** Do you seek a good conversationalist, a debater, a good listener, someone you feel safe and comfortable with? (Many happy couples recall that when they first met, they talked for hours.)

___ **Religion:** How important are religious affiliation, spiritual beliefs, and holiday celebrations to you?

___ **Intelligence:** How smart a person do you see yourself with? (People tend to feel most compatible with other people of comparable intelligence.)

___ **Education level:** How important is a college degree, a graduate degree?

___ **Family background:** What kind of family background would make you most comfortable? A certain ethnic or educational background? Close-knit or more distant? Large or small family?

___ **Politics and community service:** Do you share these convictions?

___ **Habits:** Does it bother you if someone is too sloppy? Too neat? How do you feel about smoking, drinking, TV watching? What habits would make you happy and comfortable; which have the opposite effect?

___ **Children:** Are you clear about finding a partner who wants to start a family—or doesn't? If you meet someone who already has children, how would you feel about that?

___ **Occupation:** Is it important to you that your partner is a professional, a businessperson, a member of the military, arts, or sports worlds?

___ **Finances:** Do you have expectations about your partner's financial background or resources?

___ **Lifestyle:** What kind of style of living and taste do you seek in a partner? How much does it matter to you?

___ **Other:**

Beth felt the same. "He was attractive to me, and the family values were there. We both came from the same kinds of close-knit families and we both knew we wanted children right away. He was the kind of person I knew I would like as a husband—he was honest and caring and a really good person. We both respected each other. And it's stayed that way. We're not just spouses, we're great friends and lovers."

2. What Strategies Will You Use to Meet a Great Partner?

The simplest and truest advice for finding a great partner is this: Go where your interests and heart take you. If you follow your interests, or develop new ones, you are most likely to meet someone who shares those interests. At the same time, you'll be going to places where you will have fun and feel inspired. That alone will put you in the best possible state of mind when the right person appears in your life.

Be prepared to devote time and energy to the process. Like an education or a career, dating with purpose takes commitment. Be willing to try something new—a new approach, a new city, a new job. It may take you dozens and dozens of dates and many months to meet your match.

The suggestions below are a good way to start or expand your search. And remember, the more open and ready you are, the easier it will be to recognize and attract the right person for you. The whole process should be exciting and fun if the marriage that could result is to be fun, too.

The simplest and truest advice for finding a great partner is this: Go where your interests and heart take you.

CONSIDER ONLINE DATING SITES, PERSONAL ADS IN MAGAZINES, AND MATCHMAKING SERVICES

Today, dating services have become the norm for people of all ages and interests, just as dances and blind dates were the way to meet people a generation or two ago. From online dating to advertising in the personals sections of magazines and local newspapers, to speed dating sessions, there are structured ways to meet a large pool of eligible partners. These relatively new approaches have led to many happy relationships and marriages.

According to Joanna, who met the love of her life on a dating service, the big advantage of the Internet is that it lets you reveal your true self much more quickly. You get down to what counts.

"Online, you're more uninhibited about yourself and can get to know a person faster and better because you are sharing your thoughts and feelings with someone before actually physically meeting them. You feel less self-conscious and end up sharing the real you with that person, not trying to be something you're not. People say we're perfectly matched, and because of our success, other people we know are trying it."

There is nothing "wrong" or embarrassing about trying these approaches.

Adam and Katie are firm believers in personal ads—that's how they met. "I had two young children, so I couldn't go out on the dating scene," says Katie. "When I read his ad in *New York Magazine* and it said, 'Doctor who likes children,' I responded immediately. That was nine years ago—and we have been happily married ever since."

If you are interested in the most popular online dating Web sites, and how to get started, as well as the benefits, the drawbacks, and some cautions to keep in mind, turn to "A Dating Primer" (p. 157).

LET FAMILY AND FRIENDS KNOW YOU ARE SERIOUSLY LOOKING

People often feel the greatest level of comfort meeting new people who are somehow connected to their circle of family and friends. It means that someone already knows them, their background, and, on some level, can vouch for them. Reconnect with high school and college friends. They usually know you well and will want the best for you. Spread the word to your current network and nag a little to make sure they follow up, no matter how hard it might be to ask.

GO OUT, DON'T SIT AT HOME

Go to family events, weddings, anniversaries, holiday parties, re-unions, neighborhood gatherings. Any celebratory event organized around a person, event, or cause is a great setting to meet someone new.

LOOK AROUND AT WORK—BUT BE CAREFUL

Many people find wonderful partners at work. Be sure to attend company parties and events. If you're not at a job where there are a number of like-minded people your age, think about changing companies. You'd be amazed at how many people find their soul mates at work. After all, you start off knowing that you have job interests and a group of co-workers in common.

Francine and Donald met at work thirteen years ago and married 100 days later. "I was absolutely sure from the beginning—I went home that weekend and told my mother that I'd met a girl who just started working in my office, and I was going to marry her," says Donald.

"It took me a couple of weeks more, because I had to settle in to the new job," says Francine. "I think I knew the day we went walking in Greenwich Village sharing a Dove Bar, which we jokingly called a Love Bar. I was trying to give him a bite and I accidentally got ice cream on his nose. We didn't have a napkin so I licked it off. I think that's when we knew it was serious. You can't be doing that with someone you're not serious about."

There are pitfalls to dating someone on the job. If the relationship doesn't work out, do you really want to be reminded of it every day in the office? Even if things go well in the relationship, there can be career difficulties. Many companies have rules against allowing one relative or spouse to report to the other. So one of you may have to move to a different job in the company—or be forced to quit. If you really meet your lifetime partner, it will all have been worth it.

ATTEND PROGRAMS AT LOCAL HOUSES OF WORSHIP

Your chances for meeting people who share your background, values, and interests at churches, synagogues, and other religious settings are very high. Many houses of worship organize social events for singles. You don't need to be a particularly interested in practicing religion. These are great place to meet compatible people and everyone is usually welcome.

JOIN A HEALTH CLUB OR GYM

You'll get fit and you'll meet new people who are also interested in health and fitness. Try a class—the barriers often come down more easily among people who have been working hard together. Hang out at the juice bar. Check out the bulletin boards—many clubs organize dances, sports trips, and other special outings for members, often clearly designating "singles" events.

TAKE A CLASS

If you're out of college, consider going for an advanced degree or enrolling in an adult class on something you love. Try a course on cooking, dancing the tango, introductory Italian, or modern art. Look for a class where there's a chance to interact with your fellow students.

JOIN YOUR HIGH SCHOOL OR COLLEGE ALUMNI CLUB

Most colleges and universities schedule lectures, wine tastings, and travel tours where you can run into old friends, or maybe old flames who got away but are now divorced and free. You can also make new friends with those who have similar interests and a sense of shared history. In addition to regular mailing lists, they usually have online postings of events as well.

PARTICIPATE IN CLUBS FOR TRAVEL, SPORT, POLITICS, MUSIC

Follow your passion. Join a sports club devoted to something you enjoy: tennis, bowling, golf, downhill or cross-country skiing, dancing, or river rafting. Look in your phone book, the local paper, or check online listings and your Chamber of Commerce for classes and events at nearby colleges, universities, park districts, community centers, Y's, and museums. Look into hiking, biking, and camping organizations that plan weekend outings. Attend concerts, author readings, museums, walking tours, plays—alone or with a friend.

VOLUNTEER

When you volunteer for a good cause, you not only do good for others, you also do good for yourself. Even if you've been feeling down about not meeting someone special, or if you're still recovering from a recent breakup, reaching out to others makes us feel great about ourselves. Moreover, when we're immersed in a meaningful activity we often make meaningful and relaxed connections with the people around us. You may just meet a like-minded person who is as kind-hearted and generous as you are.

SUPERMARKETS CAN BE SINGLES HANGOUTS

In many cities, certain supermarkets are famous for being places to meet other singles. If you're single, chances are you have to go grocery shopping sooner or later. Even if your local grocery store isn't known as a singles haven, it can pay to keep your eyes peeled for dating prospects.

BARS ARE OKAY, BUT NOT IDEAL

Though many people do meet in bars, these encounters are often not the most opportune. First, the lighting isn't great, so you can't really see whom you're talking to. Second, the surroundings tend to be noisy, so it's hard to carry on a conversation that would really let you know much about the other person. The mood can also be one of forced gaiety, making it less likely for either of you to reveal much about yourselves.

Meeting the right person sometimes requires a radical change in your life. It's a daring option, but it might be just what you need.

CONSIDER A RADICAL CHANGE IN YOUR LIFE

Meeting the right person sometimes requires a radical change in your life. That may mean changing the place where you live, changing your profession, or changing jobs. Each step gives you a new perspective, new goals, and a new environment, and having made that decision will make other decisions easier. It's a daring option, but it might be just what you need.

Gwendolyn, a successful advertising executive living in her hometown of Chicago, was in a six-year relationship, but she felt it was going nowhere. One day she said to her mother, "You know, I've always wanted to be a pediatrician. Too bad I never did that." Her mother answered, "Why don't you try that now?" "But Mom," Gwen said, "I'm twenty-seven years old. I'll be thirty-five by the time I graduate from medical school." Her mother's answer was, "You'll be thirty-five anyway, so why not go to medical school and be what you really want to be?"

Gwen went to medical school, started dating in a totally new environment, and, through one of her colleagues, met an attractive man from a totally different part of the country. They were engaged a few months later, married shortly after that, and had their first child before Gwen finished medical school and their second just before she finished her residency—with her husband providing great support all the way.

None of this could have happened without a drastic change in her attitude about her life and her environment.

3. If This Is Your Second (Or Third) Marriage (Or Long-Term Relationship), What Are You Going to Do Differently?

People going into a second marriage have a very good chance for happiness if they avoid the mistakes that kept their first marriage from succeeding. Don't be discouraged by statistics. Though it is widely known that the divorce rate for second marriages is higher than for first marriages, that doesn't have to be the case for you.

There's no limit to the happiness you can find in a second marriage—if you choose the right partner for you (and for your children if you have them).

We were surprised at the number of people we interviewed with truly great second marriages who hadn't gotten it right the first time.

So often we heard, "My whole life changed with my second marriage. I didn't know I could be so happy." There's no limit to the happiness you can find in a second marriage—if you choose the right partner for you (and for your children if you have them).

But how do you protect yourself and make better decisions the second time around? For starters, take the time to analyze what went wrong with your last marriage or relationship. Don't settle for the first explanation that comes to you, and don't be satisfied with simply blaming the problem on the other person. All relationships involve two people. Try to face what part your actions, reactions, or personality might have played in the unraveling of that relationship. If you need to make changes, get the help you need to do it, whether the help is counseling or simply focusing your energy and efforts on taking a different path.

When Ellen and Evan first met, they fell so madly in love they ignored important differences in their personalities.

"In looking back, I must have been pretty bossy in our relationship," Ellen says. "Our friends called us 'The Honeydews' because I was always saying 'Honey do this' or 'Honey do that.'

"My mother had died when I was seventeen, and I learned to become independent and shift for myself. I had my own apartment, took care of my younger brother, and earned my own living. Evan, on the other hand, never lived on his own. He lived with his father until we got married, and then he moved into my apartment.

"After twenty years, Evan got fed up and walked out. I was devastated. I cried for the better part of a year.

"Then one day I met Harry. I could tell immediately that here was a man who could stand up to me. And I respected that. At the same time, he was gentle and respectful of me, too. We've had twenty wonderful years together."

Develop new routines and rituals that are unique to the two of you—and different from those you practiced in your previous relationship. Consider living someplace new or even changing jobs. If part of the problem in your first marriage was your partner's traits or actions, make sure you pay close attention to your new partner's behavioral and emotional makeup. For example, if you thought you wanted a "strong" person and only later realized that the strength that attracted you turned out to be a controlling or domineering personality, make sure your next partner shows you the respect you deserve. If your last partner was unfaithful, you need to make clear to any new partner that such behavior is unacceptable in the kind of marriage you want.

Doris made some serious changes the second time around. "I was married to a very successful man who felt strongly about being in control of everything in our lives, all the time. When the kids finished high school, he divorced me. It turned out to be the best thing that ever happened to me. I met Joel a few years later, and my life changed. He respects and admires me—and I feel the same way about him. He has given me the freedom to grow. He has encouraged talents I hadn't known I had. I became an artist and I even have gallery shows. Being together changed his life as well. Now we share decisions and we share many of the same passions. I didn't know I could be this happy."

4. If You Are Dating Someone Casually, When Is It Time for Greater Commitment?

If you liked the first few weeks or months of casual dating with someone special, you may be asking yourself, "Should we get serious? And what does that mean?"

Serious dating does not have to mean you are ready to get married. It does mean that somewhere in your mind you do not rule out the possibility of marriage with this partner and would like to see where you are both headed.

EXCLUSIVITY IS THE FIRST STEP

The sign that you are ready to move from casual dating to serious dating is a simple one: you are dating each other exclusively because neither one of you wants to date anyone else. It may not come about as a conscious decision at first. It may evolve naturally. You both are so happy about seeing each other—and so unhappy when apart—that you are not really interested in seeing anyone else.

At some point, it will dawn on both of you that you are too wrapped up in the relationship to date anyone else. When that realization hits—and you both consciously agree to that exclusivity—

you are dating seriously.

If you have been dating exclusively for a while, you are probably asking yourself questions, such as, "Where is this relationship headed?" "How will I know if this person is really right for me?" "Are we compatible enough to continue seeing each other, or is this involvement only a pleasant way to pass the time?" If you are still a little overwhelmed by your feelings of being "in love" and you fear that your passion may be clouding your judgment, you might want a slightly more objective assessment of whether this person is truly right for you.

Remember the list you made at the beginning of this chapter of what you were looking for in a partner? You may want to refer to it once more to see how your current partner matches up to your ideal. You may also want to make some changes in how you rated that list.

Be realistic about your expectations. You may never be able to get 100 percent of the wish list. But be clear in your own mind what you are not willing to do without.

Examine all the qualities you rate as "Essential, not willing to live without." See how your partner does on those issues. Make sure you are sexually attracted to each other. If you're having sex, be sure you both enjoy it. If not, you both need to be willing to work together to make it satisfying, because it's an important part of any great marriage.

Be realistic about your expectations. You may never be able to get 100 percent of the wish list. But be clear in your own mind what you are not willing to do without.

If this relationship isn't "it," and you are serious about getting married, then you have an important decision to make. You can continue to date this "satisfactory" person, but you must face the fact that you are settling for security instead of seeking your best possible match. Or you can decide not to settle. Summon your courage to break it off with your current partner—and redirect the time and energy you would have devoted to that relationship to finding someone who will make you happy for life.

But remember that nobody is perfect, so don't expect the impossible. If you both are having a great time and have a clear idea of what you want and need, then relax. Trust your instincts that you are moving in the right direction in your quest to find an exceptional partner.

DECIDING TO LIVE TOGETHER

There is no magic answer, but research suggests that couples who date seriously for one or two years before marriage are more likely to have lasting marriages than those who date only a very short time. If you have dated lots of people over the years, you may be much clearer on what you want and need in a lifetime partner.

We all know couples who dated a matter of weeks, like we did, decided they had found "the one for them," and proceeded quickly to a long and happy marriage. But we also know many couples who did the same and ended up divorced.

As in most things in life, good judgment is the key. Dating for a reasonable period of time—not too long or too short—gives you the best chance for finding out just how compatible you are with each other. If you both are completely certain that you are right for each other, this might be the time for you to get engaged or consider living together. Nearly 60 percent of couples today live together at some point before marriage, compared to only 10 percent forty years ago.

LIVING TOGETHER FOR THE RIGHT REASONS

If you are serious about the relationship, moving in together may seem like a "trial marriage," as suggested by the famous anthropologist Margaret Mead. It is a time to keep house together, support each other, solve problems together, get to know each other better than ever, and get ready for a lifetime commitment. How well you handle this new stage in your relationship will set the tone for your life together. If you do it well, it could be the basis of a great marriage. If your life together is not great, you will learn that, too, from this trial period.

You will get the most out of living together if you take that step for the right reasons:

REALITY CHECK: LOOK OUT FOR FOURTEEN "FATAL FLAWS" AND UNACCEPTABLE BEHAVIOR IN A PARTNER

If your relationship is getting more serious, it is very important to pay attention to troublesome behavioral and emotional problems that could create serious problems in a long-term relationship. No matter how attractive your partner seems to be, don't dismiss character and relationship problems, even if you're totally caught up in the romance or feeling desperate for a partner. Here are telltale behaviors to watch out for:

- Addiction or excessive use of alcohol, pills, drugs, gambling, etc.
- Controlling or bullying tendencies
- Dishonesty, lying
- Displays of contempt, condescension, and overall lack of respect
- Emotional withdrawal (inability to express emotions)
- Excessive or explosive anger
- Extreme defensiveness or denial that obstructs open discussion
- Frequent critical, demeaning, or insulting remarks
- Infidelity
- Intolerance or excessive rigidity
- Laziness and unwillingness to do his/her share
- Rudeness, bad manners
- Selfishness or inability to show kindness, caring, and support
- Violence or verbal abuse

Don't compromise. These are areas that must be resolved before marriage. Living together and getting married will not change anything. Only the person with these behavior problems can change him or herself. This is not the time to compromise. Unless your partner sees a therapist or participates in couples or group counseling to resolve the problem behavior, your relationship is headed for trouble. If you're not sure your concerns are warranted, you can explore them further in the discussion of acceptable behaviors in Chapter Four, "Agree on the Big Six" (p. 59), and perhaps discuss them with a professional.

- You both love each other and think you want to be together forever, but you want to experience a preview of what life together will be like and see how comfortably you can both adjust to each other's habits and lifestyles.
- You want to make sure you agree on the important issues—the Big Six—of religion, money, sex, children, recreation, and acceptable behavior. Living together will afford you time and space to go into those intimate discussions with each other to make sure you can have a great marriage together. (See Chapter Four, "Agree on the Big Six" [p. 59], for an in-depth exploration of these critical areas.)

LIVING TOGETHER FOR THE WRONG REASONS

Be cautious, however, if you are thinking of living together for the wrong reasons. You can slip into living together for reasons that sound practical and convenient but will probably not move you any closer to a great marriage. As pleasant, exciting, or safe as moving in together might seem, it may actually keep you from finding "the real thing."

A "*yes*" answer to any of these statements indicates a less than good enough reason to live together:

- "I know this isn't perfect, but I can't face going back to dating."
- "We'll save on the rent, and I won't have to live alone anymore."
- "We love being together, but we're not ready to make the leap to marriage."
- "We spend so much time together, we may as well live together."
- "I don't want to hurt his/her feelings, and he/she seems to think it's a good idea."
- "We *think* things are going well, but we want to keep a closer watch on some behavior issues before we decide if this is 'for keeps.'"
- "I don't want to start all over with someone new. If we move in together, we can see what happens."
- "We've been together for a long time, so we guess it's time to take it to the next level. Otherwise our relationship will never go anywhere."
- "Maybe he/she will change if we live together."

HOW SERIOUS IS YOUR RELATIONSHIP?

Here's how to tell if you should take this relationship to the next level.

- *You are having a great time, and are convinced that this partner is marriage material*. Yes? Congratulations. But if that's not how you feel, it may be time to start looking again. Sure, that takes courage and effort. But recognize that devoting time to sustaining this mediocre relationship takes your energy and attention away from finding a truly great lifetime partner.
- *You feel as if you are having a great time together, are very comfortable, and are sure that what you two have is truly love.* Yes? Great. If not, keep on dating. Look at your compatibility list and ask yourself, "Does this person make me happy? Do I make this person happy? Have I considered serious behavioral and emotional issues that could get in the way? (See "Reality Check" on page 42.)
- *You can't wait until the next time you see each other again, and the prospect of doing nothing together sounds better than doing most anything with anybody else.* Yes? Wonderful. If not, keep on dating and see how things proceed.

If you can answer "yes" to all three questions, and you feel that you could happily live with each other for the rest of your lives, these are very good signs that you may be right for each other. Consider lgetting engaged and/or moving in together as a next step.

When you date with purpose and find the right partner, you will find not only that you love your partner but that your partner makes you feel loved, too. You will find the kind of deep love that will be built on a strong foundation and bring you both joy for a lifetime.

When you date with purpose and find the right partner, you will find not only that you love your partner but that your partner makes you feel loved, too.

PART TWO

Starting a Great Relationship

CHAPTER THREE

Put Love and Respect First: Bring Out the Best in Each Other

To love someone deeply gives you strength.
Being loved by someone deeply gives you courage.

—Lao Tzu

ONE OF OUR CLOSEST FRIENDS WAS GIVING a talk at a local fundraiser. After her speech, she was asked what she thought was the key to her happy marriage of more than fifty years. She said, "I have two words: love and respect."

And we couldn't agree more. The reason our friend's marriage has lasted more than fifty years is because both she and her husband not only feel love and respect for each other, they show it to each other as well. Every day. In big ways and small.

If you want a relationship to last, you have to focus on what you both have in common, not on what divides you, what you admire in each other, not what you might want to criticize. Notice what you like about your partner—and let your partner know. Encourage each other to become the kind of people you both respect and admire. Bring out the best in each other. Then tell each other how good you feel about being together.

Kathryn and Roger, married eight years, are both on their second—and much happier—marriage.

"In my first marriage, I didn't realize how important respect and admiration were to a lasting relationship, because I never felt like I got any," says Kathryn. "But this marriage is so different—it's like night and day. I didn't know how good it would feel to have someone admire me—and for me to feel the same about him. I have so much respect for Roger's kindness."

Roger continues: "And I really admire Kathryn's skills. She is intelligent, and I have a lot of respect for her ideas. She's also a great cook, and she's so organized," Roger adds. "My first marriage wasn't anything like this."

If you want a relationship to last, you have to focus on what you both have in common, not on what divides you. Notice what you like about your partner—and let your partner know.

Speak Lovingly

Though there are many ways to build your love, you cannot go wrong if you start by speaking lovingly to each other. Using a loving tone to comment on the simplest of daily events can make your partner feel wonderful. "Dinner was great." "I'm so glad you called me at work today—I really needed that boost." "That was fun last night, let's do it again soon." "Everybody admired how you handled those questions at the meeting yesterday." "Your suggestions for how to handle the kids worked out really well."

As you talk to each other and get to know each other better, don't forget that it is as important a sign of respect to listen as it is to speak up about your own inner thoughts and feelings. As Paul Tillich, the great theologian, said: "The first duty of love is to listen."

Show Your Respect

There's no better way to show respect for your partner's opinion than by asking for advice—and, if possible, heeding it. Indirect approaches can work, too. Let him carry out tasks his own way—without butting in or offering unsolicited advice. Let her make decisions on matters she cares more deeply about, even if you think there's a better way.

There's no better way to show respect for your partner's opinion than by asking for advice—and, if possible, heeding it.

Notice things your partner does well—or that you do well together. If you really want to demonstrate your respect and admiration, tell others about the things your partner has done well. Show that you believe your partner deserves everyone's admiration, not just yours.

Express Appreciation and Gratitude

To make your relationship sweet, go out of your way to notice the small things you each do to help and support one another—and express your thanks. Show your gratitude for even the small gestures; it's another way of expressing your love. If you both show your appreciation and gratitude for the small acts of kindness, you will find yourselves falling in love over and over again.

Be Kind and Understanding

Happy couples say it is important not only to show your kindness to the world, but also to each other. Often it's the little things that count.

"My wife's best friend had to go into the hospital suddenly a few weeks ago," recalls Edward, married nine years. "So I told her, 'You go visit her—I'll stay home from work and take care of the baby.' It meant a lot to her."

It can also apply to bigger issues.

"My husband lost his job, after ten years at the company," Sharon says. "He was feeling a little panicky about our financial situation. But we sat down and talked, and I told him, 'Honey, don't take the first thing that comes along. We'll manage. I don't mind working overtime for a while, until you find what you really want.'"

Put yourself in your partner's shoes. If you notice he or she is troubled or upset by something, draw your partner out to find out why. Make time to talk about things that are important to your partner—and to both of you. Show empathy. Even if you feel as if your partner has been responsible for a problem that has come up, try asking yourself how you might make changes to improve things, instead of asking, "What did my partner do wrong and how can he or she fix it?" As Ben Franklin said, "If you would be loved, love and be loveable."

Put Your Partner First

Make it a habit to put your partner's best interests first. It's not as hard as it sounds: every time you need to make a significant decision, each of you should ask yourself, "How will my partner feel about this? Will this be good for my partner?" Whenever possible, include your partner in the decision making.

Every time you need to make a significant decision, each of you should ask yourself, "How will my partner feel about this? Will this be good for my partner?"

If you are sensitive to each other's needs and wants, you will bring out the best in each other, and provide for each other's needs without sacrificing your own.

During Henry and Jillian's tenth year of marriage they decided to move to a larger apartment, which had two extra bedrooms that they could use for private offices. "We had endless debates over who would get the larger office," says Henry. "Finally I won the debate. Jillian agreed to do it my way: She let me take the smaller office."

Be Affectionate—Touch Each Other

Touch each other lovingly and often, even when you have no intention of that gesture leading to sex. Just as infants will only grow and flourish if they are held and touched, so couples need physical affection for their relationship and marriage to thrive. Keeping in touch physically is as important as keeping in touch by phone or e-mail when you are apart.

Make a date and go out at least once a week—just the two of you. Have romantic dinners together. Go dancing, to the movies, or just pick a place where you can talk quietly and connect. Make the planning and anticipation of your vacations as much fun as the vacation itself. Celebrate your being together, every day.

Be generous with your hugs and kisses and touches. Don't let your loving ways change once you are married. Leave little love notes in unexpected places. Wear clothes your partner likes. Make going to bed each evening a special ritual so you can kiss and feel close before falling asleep. The more affectionate you are routinely, the more you both will enjoy the love, commitment, and passion that flows from that affection.

Show Love through Passion

Both of you should make sex a top priority, with each of you aiming to delight and satisfy the other. If the sex is not yet what you both would like it to be, work on it lovingly together until it is. Explore good books on sex together (see "Recommended Reading," page 181), rent helpful videos, go to lectures or retreats that will expand your lovemaking pleasure. Talk gently about your wants and needs; listen carefully to those of your partner. Draw strength from this pleasurable way of relating to each other. As Samuel Johnson said, "Marriage has many pains, but celibacy has no pleasures."

Harry and Joyce, married thirty-two years, say sex has gotten better and better over the years. "I know what turns her on now and what she needs," says Harry. "And I'm probably more relaxed now than when I was younger and more willing to try things," says Joyce. "I guess that has made it a lot more fun."

Forge Loving Rituals

Humans define themselves by their commitments—they are part of who we are and how we see ourselves. Take satisfaction in the feeling of security that commitment can give you both as you work your way through some of the adjustments you may have to make as a couple, especially in the early stages of living together and marriage.

Initiate new rituals that belong to just the two of you. Light a candle at dinner, call each other private nicknames, make a cup of coffee and read aloud to each other from your favorite novel or collection of poetry, have breakfast in bed on Sundays and agree not to talk about chores, conflicts, or problems of any sort for those two hours. Shared rituals connect you and bring you closer.

Stay in touch with your partner's daily life. Before you rush off in the morning, make sure to tell each other at least one thing you plan to do during the day so you both feel connected even when you're apart. When you return in the evening, follow up and find out how that activity or event went. It shows you care about your partner's life and gives you something of interest to discuss at the dinner table.

"We alternate making tea and toast for each other every morning," says Peter and Sarah, who met in Chicago and now live in Denver. "When I told my mother about our morning ritual she said, 'That's cute; I wonder how long that will last?' Well, it's thirty years later, and we're still doing it."

Look for little things you can do together on occasion—fold the laundry or make the bed together. Even if it might be more efficient to carry out those chores separately, it reminds you that you are now a team.

"We make the bed together almost every morning," Alan says. "I always try to give her a little more of the sheet on her side, for comfort," Alan says. Sylvia adds: "I do the same. It reminds us each day, how much we care about each other and how well we work together."

Build Trust and Respect with Honesty

It is crucial to be honest with each other—that is how you build trust and demonstrate your respect. You have to be able to count on each other's word to not only tell the truth but also carry out promises.

If something is really wrong at work, for example, and you say, "Nothing is wrong," you are doing yourself and your partner a disservice by being dishonest. You need to be candid and open even if it takes courage to level with your spouse.

Be Tactful

Although honesty is the best policy, it is equally important to be tactful. There are some sensitive areas where it is probably better to suspend judgment, or at least hold your tongue. Weight issues, birthday presents, the handling of difficult relatives, and new dinner recipes that may not always turn out as deliciously as everyone hoped are common topics where you should exercise caution and tact.

Politeness counts, too. Even though many newlyweds are tempted to drop some of the polite gestures as they start feeling closer and more at ease with each other, happy couples say that would be a mistake. Politeness doesn't mean being stuffy or formal. On the contrary, it shows how much you care about and respect your partner, and can only bring you closer.

Be Faithful

You must be able to trust each other completely. Happy couples say they never want to make their partner feel insecure about their love. They never behave in any way to give their loved one reason to doubt their loyalty. If you can't trust each other to remain faithful, it is very difficult to trust each other about anything else.

Being faithful is an attitude as much as an action. Staying faithful is a way of saying, "I love you, and I have made a commitment that I'm going to stick with. I will stay away from any temptation that might come my way." It is not enough to be faithful. You have to make sure not to give the appearance that you are anything but faithful. That means you never act like you're interested in anyone else romantically. And you don't do anything in public or private that you wouldn't want your partner to see or know about.

Staying faithful is a way of saying, "I love you, and I have made a commitment that I'm going to stick with." Don't do anything in public or private that you wouldn't want your partner to see or know about.

Be Positive

Seeing the world in a positive light is as much a matter of habit as it is a function of personality. Even if you don't see yourself as an optimistic person, you can change some daily habits to move you in that direction. It's worth the effort—you both will benefit by keeping things positive.

Celebrate your similarities and shared values. Remind yourself each day to look for what you and your partner agree upon and have in common, instead of focusing on your differences. Don't dwell on things that could go wrong. Focus on what you can do to make things go right.

Look for the positive in your partner's personality and in your daily interactions together. Give voice to these positive observations on a regular basis. Try to keep little criticisms to yourself. Happy couples make a lot more positive statements than negative ones about each other, by a ratio of 5 to 1, according to researchers.

You may feel self-conscious at the start, but once you get in the habit of looking for the positive side of things, you'll see what a difference you can make. You'll not only improve your own mood by finding so much to feel good about, but you will lift your partner's spirits, too.

Use Humor Lovingly

You don't have to start memorizing jokes. But if you look at the world and your relationship with an eye to the humor that can be found in even difficult situations, you will find it cuts the tension and promotes warm, loving feelings between you. Sharing laughter is a sign that you trust each other enough to let down your guard. Laughter is, indeed, one of the best love medicines for a great marriage.

Be Flexible about Each Other's Habits and Temperament

Everyone has some quirks. One person is bound to be neater than the other or more punctual. One of you may be more of a morning person or a night person. You may need different amounts of sleep. You may have different priorities about what kind of furniture belongs in your home or how to spend your free time.

Look upon these differences as interesting discoveries, not potential time bombs. Remove irritants. Small habits can be changed, especially if both of you remember your aim is to make the other happy. Those habits that cannot be changed can often be worked around. Using separate tubes of toothpaste is far easier than fighting about the caps. Many disagreements are that easily solved, with the right attitude.

Using separate tubes of toothpaste is far easier than fighting about the caps. Many disagreements are that easily solved, with the right attitude.

Be tolerant of each other's faults. It is perfectly reasonable to ask for some changes of habits that bother you. But be prepared to do the same for your spouse. If you're an early bird, let your lover sleep in. If eating dinner together matters to your mate, get to work early so you can make it home on time. Be patient. And learn when to let the small things go.

When you both have different ideas on what to do, find a new solution that you both can love—and live with. Don't try to compromise with a solution that doesn't make either one of you really happy. If one of you wants to go for a bike ride and the other wants to watch a football game on TV, probably neither of you will be happy spending an hour at each. It's often better to come up with a third way—an entirely new plan of action—go for a walk or go out for a cocktail—that is more likely to make both of you happy. Don't give up, even if you can't set things right every time. Keep trying to make your partner happy; it will pay off in happiness for you, too.

"Gerry and I learned the art of finding happy solutions to conflicts early and practiced it all our lives," Lilo says. "For our twenty-fifth anniversary, our children got us an expensive bicycle built for two. As soon as we got on it, we realized that neither one of us was willing to sit in back and have no control over where we were going. We didn't think it would be a good solution to trade off—with each of us spending only half the time in back. All that would have meant is that each of us was unhappy half the time.

"So we decided to trade the bike in for two mopeds—one for each of us. When we decided we really wanted more exercise, we traded in the mopeds for mountain bikes. That made us both happy—and it made our kids happy, too."

Take Time to Play Together

Play is often what brings you together in the first place—and it can keep you together, too. Do things together that you both like to do in your leisure time. Discover new activities that you can enjoy together—a new sport or perhaps travel to far places neither of you has ever seen. Suggest activities that you know your partner loves doing, like watching a baseball game or going to a dance or a museum, even if it's not your favorite pastime.

Take walks together, make dinner as a team, meet with friends, cuddle up and read the newspaper. Having fun playing together solidifies your bonds as surely as working together does—maybe even more so. Relaxing and playing together also builds loving memories for life.

Respect Each Other's Privacy

When you go from being two independent singles to one couple sharing everything, you may feel as if you have lost some freedom. That just goes with the territory. As Linda recalled about her first year of marriage, soon after she and her partner signed the lease on their new apartment in Chicago: "The hardest part of living together was having to tell someone where I was going all the time. I was no longer free to come and go as I pleased."

You will also feel as if you have much less privacy. Your mail is no longer for your eyes only. The same goes for your phone calls.

Hard as these changes may seem, working through them will bring you closer. Agree that you will honor each other's privacy— leave each other's messages on the answering machine, don't open each other's mail. But share the messages and the news, so you don't have secrets from each other. Treat each other respectfully, communicating what you want or need without criticizing. This applies to even the smallest issues, such as leaving the bathroom door open or closed, allocating shelf space for toiletries. Each small accommodation provides a chance to show each other how much you care.

Give Each Other Some Time Alone

"Let there be spaces in your togetherness," Kahlil Gibran wrote in *The Prophet*. As important as it is to do things together, it is equally important for each of you to be free to do things on your own. Most people need some time to be alone to think, work, listen to music, read a book, talk to a friend, in short, to "refuel" their personal resources.

You show trust and respect for your partner's independence by giving him or her the gift of time alone. As Marnie Reed Crowell wrote in *Green Pastures*: "To keep the fire burning brightly there's one easy rule: Keep the two logs together, near enough to keep each other warm and far enough apart—about a finger's breadth—for breathing room. Good fire, good marriage, same rule."

Get to Know Each Other's Friends and Family

Show your love and respect for your partner by your willingness to extend those feelings to the people he or she cares for most. Try to be open and accepting, not judgmental or critical. When you get to know your partner's friends and family members, look for the same positive things he or she sees in them so you can make them your friends and family, too. Make new friends together, too. After all, if this relationship is to blossom over the years, this expanded network will be an important source of love and support for both of you.

Explore Each Other's Dreams and Aspirations

Talk about your hopes and dreams. Encourage your partner to do the same. Show respect and encouragement for each other as you work toward those dreams.

Let your partner know you understand and admire who he is now and who he wants to become. Let her know you trust her judgment and respect her dreams for the future. All of us, no matter how confident or accomplished we may appear on the outside, want to be understood and need to be reassured that our partner not only "gets" us, but approves of us as well.

Don't Do the Things That Drive Your Partner Crazy

You know what this means. As you get to know each other better, you learn what your partner likes and dislikes, what the "hot buttons" are. All of us have some issues that may or may not be rational, but that drive us up the wall. It may be something your partner says, or some clothing he wears, or the way she acts in a particular situation. Perhaps you know that being late makes your partner see red, or drinking juice straight from the container drives your mate crazy. Don't push those buttons.

Don't do the things that drive your partner crazy.

Your job is to make your partner happy—and encourage your partner to do the same for you. Leave the buttons alone.

Do Everything with Love

Sometimes it's just that simple. Be loving and be consistent about it. Admit it when you are wrong. And forgive your partner when he or she turns out to be wrong. Who among us is perfect?

A great marriage is not a matter of luck—though you may both feel very lucky to have met each other. Sustaining a relationship is a product of careful thought, a generous spirit, and hard work. Fortunately, all the hard work you do will bring impressive results. Your love and respect and caring behavior can lead to a profoundly satisfying intimacy and pleasure that only an exceptional, lifelong marriage can bring.

CHAPTER FOUR

Agree on the Big Six: Religion, Money, Sex, Children, Recreation, and Acceptable Behavior

There is nothing nobler or more admirable than when two people who see eye to eye keep house as man and wife, confounding their enemies and delighting their friends.

—HOMER, *The Odyssey*

MANY PEOPLE DO NOT REALIZE HOW IMPORTANT it is for two loving partners to "see eye to eye" on religion, money, sex, children, recreation, and acceptable behavior for their future lives together. That's why we call them the Big Six. These are the essential issues that couples must come to agreement on at an early stage of a serious relationship.

If you're in a relatively new relationship, you may feel anxious or afraid to bring up any potentially volatile subjects. You may have a strong desire to maintain your shared sense of optimism and harmony. You may believe that he is a wonderful man, or that she is the most intriguing woman you've ever met.

But the Big Six are not issues you can ignore. They will not simply "work themselves out," as many couples mistakenly hope. Without full agreement on each of these issues in a way that makes both of you happy, your marriage will not be built on a solid foundation.

Your goal is not to avoid differences. For many people, differences in race, ethnicity, religion, social background, and the like, can be very attractive features in a partner. What you want to do is talk over any differences you may have and resolve how you will handle them *before* you marry.

Your goal is not to avoid differences. What you want to do is talk over any differences you may have and resolve how you will handle them *before* you marry.

If your long-term relationship is at a standstill, or has some serious conflicts, it can be very helpful to review these six issues. It may be that unresolved differences on these matters are underlying some of your uncertainty or unhappiness. Focusing on specific concerns can take some of the tension out of your discussions and may lead you to a clearer picture of what's coming between you.

Whichever stage you find yourselves in, you have two options:

- You can keep trying to resolve your issues: Look for a new approach you haven't considered before, seek counseling or outside help. See if you can come to an agreement or change behavior in a way that pleases you both.
- You can part ways: It is best to listen to your inner voice, the one that guides your hunches and instincts. If you part ways, hard as that may seem, it opens up an opportunity to find the right partner who does agree with you on all of these six critical issues.

1. Religion

In today's global and mobile world, it isn't surprising that many couples come from different regions and religions. In great marriages, both partners do not need to share identical religious backgrounds as long as they feel in harmony about the part religion will (or will not) play in the life they are creating together.

"One of the craziest things I can say is that even though I consider

---

THE BIG SIX

1. **Religion:** You have to agree on and feel comfortable with what role religion plays in your lives, and how you will raise the children, if any.
2. **Money:** You have to share common views on money—how you'll earn it, save it, and spend it.
3. **Sex:** You both have to enjoy sex together and feel that sex between you is important and great—and be willing to make it even better.
4. **Children:** You need to agree on whether you plan to have children, when, how many, how and where you plan to raise them, and what to do if you can't have them.
5. **Recreation:** You have to share ideas about how you will spend your time together—what recreational activities you both enjoy—and how you'll sometimes spend your time on your own.
6. **Acceptable behavior:** You have to be totally comfortable with each other's behavior and agree on what is acceptable—and what is not.

---

myself more devout than Donald, the way that Donald lives his life, he's so ethical he's almost more religious than I am," says Francine about her husband of thirteen years. They married each other first in City Hall and then in a church ceremony a year later. "I have tremendous respect for him. He definitely gets the difference between right and wrong."

For many of us, religious beliefs are deeply imbedded in our identities, but we may not realize just how strongly we feel. Religion doesn't necessarily pop up in casual conversation in the early stages of a relationship. Certainly not as often as, say, your preferences about food or movies. Some people may not realize how important their religious beliefs are until they are planning who will officiate at the wedding service—or until they think about what kind of religious teaching, if any, they might want for their children. It's one thing to agree about going together or separately to religious services; it can be quite another to decide which religion the children will practice.

Here are common scenarios that may fit your circumstances and help you come to an agreement about how you'll handle religion in your lives.

SAME RELIGIOUS VIEWS

Even if you both share the same religion, or share the belief that religion is not important in your lives, you still need to have this critical discussion together. You may both call yourselves Catholic or Jewish or Protestant or Muslim or agnostic or atheist, but you may have very different ideas about the role your religion will play in your daily living and on holidays. You need to find out if you agree on the details. How observant are each of you? Will you join a religious institution? Do you expect your partner to come to services with you? How do you plan to raise the children? Who will instruct them and in which branch of which religion?

DIFFERENT RELIGIONS, ONE PARTNER CONVERTS

If you come from different religious backgrounds, as many successful couples do, you have to discuss how you each plan to practice religion in your life together. When one partner converts, that usually resolves the differences and answers the question about how the children will be raised.

DIFFERENT RELIGIONS, EACH PRACTICES INDEPENDENTLY

Many couples of different religions decide they can be happy allowing both partners to practice their own religion independently. But that still leaves an important discussion on what religion the children will follow. Will they be raised in your religion, your partner's, or will you familiarize them with both religions and let them decide for themselves?

ONE RELIGION CHOSEN FOR THE CHILDREN

When the parents have different religions, they may not feel it necessary for one of them to convert to create family harmony. But they often agree to raise the children with one faith.

NO RELIGION PRACTICED—LET THE CHILDREN DECIDE WHEN THEY GROW UP

If you both did not grow up with a religious faith or you both choose not to practice any faith, you may agree that it is best to let the children decide for themselves which faith, if any, to follow when they grow up.

In all of these options, the goal is to find a religious path that satisfies both your needs. (You might take a look at the section on raising children in Chapter Nine, "Enjoy Raising Children" [p. 127], to see how five happy couples managed to come to an agreement on their differing religious beliefs.)

Only when you can join forces on this issue will you be able to provide a stable environment for raising children and an enduring way to live together happily.

2. Money

At the beginning of a relationship, partners may not know what they can realistically expect to earn or how much they should allocate for housing, clothing, recreation, cars, food, and education. But partners in great marriages say that when both partners regard their contributions to the relationship and the family as equal, no matter who earns how much, tensions over money matters subside.

When problems arise, it is usually because discussions about money often are not really about money; they are just as often about control, values, goals, and dreams. When couples jointly decide and agree on the basic issues of acceptable risks to take with regard to jobs and money, when to make big expenditures, and how to handle debt and savings, they seem to manage well financially...and thrive emotionally.

When problems arise, it is usually because discussions about money often are not really about money; they are just as often about control, values, goals, and dreams.

How do you find out if you are in agreement? Ask each other some basic questions that will reveal your financial attitudes—and your financial hot buttons.

- **Earning:** How much do you expect to earn? Is it important to you to have a lot of money? What kind of lifestyle do you want to have now and ten years from now? Do you have a plan for achieving those financial goals? How would you feel if you don't reach them? Would you be willing to marry this partner if he or she earned less?
- **Spending:** How do feel about spending money? How much planning do you want to go into major purchases? Is there any kind of spending that your partner might do that would drive you crazy? What spending decisions do you think you need to share? Would you be annoyed if your partner bought new clothes each month or made risky stock market investments? Are you both willing to stick to a budget?
- **Saving:** How do you feel about saving money? Do you have common long-term goals to save money for such as starting a business, buying a house or a car, college tuition, retirement, or an emergency in one of your families? Would you be willing to plan a budget and stick to it monthly in order to save? What steps would you be willing to take in order to save more?
- **Issues from a Previous Marriage:** If one or both of you has been married before—and especially if there are children from those marriages—there are a number of legal, moral, and financial issues you'll need to discuss. For example, you may have assets from your previous marriage that have to be protected for your children or a former spouse. A prenuptial agreement may be advisable. It is very important to go over these matters together in detail so you both are comfortable with the arrangement.
- **Troubles:** How would you deal with financial adversity? If one of you became disabled and couldn't earn for a year, what would you do to adapt?
- **Family Background:** If your partner grew up in a richer family than yours, or a poorer one, how might that affect the way each of you handles money? If you each come from very different backgrounds, with a wide disparity in assets before the

marriage, it is important to talk over both of your expectations about how these previous assets will be treated within the marriage. Discuss these financial matters now so there will be no surprises and less potential for disagreements in the future.

- **Opportunity and Risk:** If there were an opportunity to make a big change, such as start a business, change professions, go back to school, or move to another city, how would you deal with it? How would you feel about financial expenditures involved with having or adopting children?
- **Debt:** How do you feel about debt? Does it scare you or your partner? Do you have credit card debt or do you pay each monthly bill in full? Do you have any other debts? If so, how are you planning to pay them off? Are you earning more than you spend or spending more than you earn?

Lilo and Gerry did not start out on exactly the same financial wavelength when they began dating. "We both vividly remember Lilo's first visit to my apartment in New York City," Gerry says. "Lilo noticed that I had left my bank statement open on the desk.

"'Why do you have some entries in red ink and others in black?' Lilo asked me. When I explained the red entries were overdrafts, Lilo said she had never heard of anyone spending more than they had in the bank—and she didn't like the idea. The solution was simple. When we got married, Lilo managed the bank account that was used to pay all the bills. We each had a separate checking account that we used only for incidentals—I used mine mostly to buy Lilo presents. We shared all our money and major financial decisions jointly. And that's the way it still is, many decades later."

If you can both agree about how to handle spending, saving, and earning the money, you will be able to smoothly manage your finances and your marriage.

Francine and Donald didn't always agree on how to spend their money. "We grew up with different philosophies," says Donald. Because she came from a poorer family than Donald, she was more inclined to look for bargains. "She didn't appreciate that if you spent a little more on furniture, it would last longer than buying cheap stuff you had to replace in a few years. So my philosophy is to wait a little longer and buy the more expensive items," explains Donald. Francine adds that after a couple of run-ins, they talked things over and she came around to his way of thinking.

3. Sexual Chemistry

In great marriages sex is a vitally important way for two partners to express and experience their love for each other. It remains a focal point of the relationship, from the time you meet until you die. Sex is both a physical and emotional bond that keeps a couple in tune and intimate. If you can't both happily envision making love to each other for the rest of your lives, you should find that out now.

"How important is sex to us? Angela can't get enough of me," says Tim, and both he and wife, Angela, crack up with laughter. After thirty-six years of marriage and five children, this New Jersey couple still clearly clicks. "About ten years ago one of our daughters was taking this health class and she wanted to know if her mom and I were equal to the national average in sex. I said, teasingly, 'Jenny, we're way above that.' I have no idea what the national average is, but sex is an important part of our marriage," Tim concludes.

Sex may not always be wonderful right from the start. But if the chemistry is there and you love each other, you can work on making it pleasurable for both of you. If sex is a new art for one or both of you, take the time to learn about it. Be patient with a partner who may not enjoy sex as much as you do for whatever reasons—inexperience or a bad previous experience. And try to avoid sexual stereotypes. Both sexes are capable of sexual desire. Both sexes can have sexual inhibitions, discomfort, and insecurity.

Sex is both a physical and emotional bond that keeps a couple in tune and intimate.

If you can't be comfortable and please each other after trying for several months, and reading books together or getting outside help— or if you don't want to bother—then maybe this is not the right relationship for you. (For suggestions to begin a discussion with your partner, read Chapter Seven, "Make Sex Great for Both of You" [p. 105], and look at the "Recommended Reading" at the end of the book.)

Connie says her sexual relationship with Bob has changed over the years—for the better. "It's a very natural, very affirming way of our being together. I had to get past some real negative attitudes about it; my Catholic education at the time was very negative and created fears. Now I understand that sex is a good way to show love and respect. We went to some marriage encounter groups, which helped. So I enjoy it a lot more now. A lot more."

4. Children

"Our children have been one of the most important parts of our marriage," says our son Richard. To have a great marriage each of you has to have some idea what kind of family you want to have—a lot of children, few children, or no children at all. You also might want to discuss where you'd like to raise your children—what part of the country, what kind of community. It may depend on the kind of family you come from. If both of you are only children, that may be what you want for yourselves. If both of you came from a large family, you both may want to duplicate that experience. Or you may want the opposite.

If you have no idea if you want a large or small family, try visiting friends and relatives with a varying number of children to see how you and your partner respond. If you don't know whether one of you will want to keep working after having children or stay home while the kids are young, talk to other new parents to see how they made those decisions.

You may not know exactly what your family plans are, but it is important to start the discussion now so you can discover if there are big issues that could divide you later. In a good relationship, where there is agreement, such discussions will only bring you closer together. Serious disagreements over whether to have children or not can put an end to an otherwise strong relationship. It's best to face this possible crossroad sooner rather than later.

Rebecca wished she had brought up the issue of children with her first serious boyfriend much earlier than she did. She had been dating Roger for five years. She had noticed his occasional disparaging remarks about infants and children, but thought he was just acting "typically macho" and trying to be funny. It wasn't until one Christmas, when they had begun talking about marriage while they were visiting another couple with a new baby, that the two of them actually had a serious talk about kids. When she learned that Roger did not want children, now or ever, she realized she had no choice.

She broke up with Roger one month later.

Three months after that, she met Bob. It didn't take long for her to find out that he loved the idea of having children as much as she did—and that was only the beginning of what they had in common. They have been very happily married for fourteen years and now have three kids, one dog, and six goldfish.

5. Recreation

One of the pillars of a great marriage is sharing common passions and pursuits, especially recreational activities and hobbies. Happy couples usually enjoy several interests that bring them together in their free time. Hiking, biking, skiing, fishing, playing tennis, baseball, working out, taking walks, reading books, or discussing movies all seem to bring them closer. They provide the couple with other ways to relate to each other—and broaden their understanding and appreciation of the other—beyond the usual world of work and home.

"We read books together; we spend so many hours talking to each other that we feel like teenagers again," say Kathryn, who is in her seventh year of marriage to Roger, after both had unhappy first marriages. Roger sums it up: "In the beginning, we had so much fun just being together we almost felt guilty."

Whether you are playing sports together, traveling, or learning something new, leisure time activities allow you both to maintain your sense of fun and recharge your marriage.

When these shared activities are active sports, they allow both partners to stay fit and healthy together. Not only does this carry the bonus of keeping them attractive to each other, it also maximizes their chances of living not simply a longer life but a better one. Both of them reap the benefits of that healthy advantage.

Playing together serves as more than a safety valve for releasing tensions productively. Sharing recreational passions provides couples with a chance to relate to each other in new ways, to admire each other for skills other than work and the daily grind. Most important, leisure activities encourage both partners to unwind, relax, stay in shape together, expand their lives together, and just have fun—all critical to building a great marriage.

Another side benefit: shared activities are just plain fun. The sign of the truly happily married couple is that they are looking for fun even when they are doing absolutely ordinary, everyday chores. Even if they don't start out with common recreational or leisure interests, couples in great marriages learn to find them.

"We do everything together," says Mark, a California lawyer who has been married to Alexis for twenty-six years. "We hike, we scuba dive, we ski, we exercise. She even comes with me to trials I have out of town," he says. "I don't know how our marriage would have survived if we couldn't have fun."

The more you can play together in your off hours, the closer you will feel. Having fun together is like an insurance policy in a marriage. It shores up those good feelings you have toward each other to help you get through the hard times.

You do not have to have *all* of your recreational interests in common. It is perfectly fine for one of you to go swimming while the other goes to a book club or visits a relative or goes to a basketball game. But the more you can play together in your off hours, the closer you will feel. Having fun together is like an insurance policy in a marriage. It shores up those good feelings you have toward each other to help you get through the hard times.

If you can't find several leisure passions you can share, your relationship may not be resilient enough to bounce back in the face of the inevitable challenges life can bring. The right person for you is a person you want to have fun with for the rest of your life.

6. Acceptable Behavior

In a great relationship or marriage, both partners behave in a way that makes the other happy without sacrificing their individual identities and values. If you demonstrate your love and respect for each other every day in words and actions, you will enjoy each other's company and find the support only a loving relationship can provide.

Yet even with the best-matched couple, there will be times when one person acts in a way that disturbs the other. If that happens only occasionally, it's not a problem. Apologize, accept the apology, go on with your lives—and try not to do it again. But if one partner's behavior regularly makes the other uncomfortable or unhappy, that cannot and should not be accepted by either. Remember, if you don't like something your partner does before you get married, you'll like it even less afterward.

Simply put, acceptable behavior makes you and your partner feel good about each other. Unacceptable behavior is any behavior that you find objectionable at the time it occurs, in the place it occurs, or with whom it occurs. Behavior becomes a problem in a relationship when it prevents one or both partners from living a healthy life or showing the consideration, kindness, and respect that the other partner deserves.

Remember, if you don't like something your partner does before you get married, you'll like it even less afterward. Simply put, acceptable behavior makes you and your partner feel good.

If you find it distasteful that your partner burps at the dinner table or uses her fingers to scoop up the peas, it is reasonable to expect that he or she can improve his or her table manners. If you curse a great deal or repeatedly forget to do your share of the chores around the house, you can learn to clean up your act, if you really want to make your partner happy. Change is possible with the proper motivation—and love is a powerful motivator. But do not expect to be able to change your partner on your own. Just think about how hard it is to change yourself. Your partner will have to want to change.

Some behaviors that will later prove unacceptable may not be obvious when you are getting to know each other. People are on their best behavior early in a relationship. Certain behaviors associated with addiction such as those involving alcohol, drugs, or gambling may seem within the normal range when a person is young. But these potential addictions can get progressively worse over time. These addictive behaviors, as well as other emotional problems such as depression, violence, or excessive anger often run in families, so it is wise to pay special attention to such worries. It is vitally important to explore the family history and get professional advice so you can both discuss your concerns. Here's a questionnaire that can help you get a better understanding of any problem behaviors in your relationship.

If your partner seems unable or unwilling to change, you have to face the possibility that such behavior may never change. The mistake many people make is to ignore the problem and say to themselves, "Oh, it'll get better once we're married." Marriage will not magically transform your partner's behavior. If a person is not motivated to make improvements at this stage, before marriage, it is unlikely he or she ever will. The longer you wait, the less likely it will be that your partner can change. If you or your partner cannot behave in a way that makes you both happy, you are not the right partners for each other.

Fourteen Problem Behaviors That Can Undermine the Best Relationship

The following checklists can help you and your partner identify possible problems and talk them over. They will also help you get to know each other better. Ask yourself and each other the following questions.

1. ADDICTION OR EXCESSIVE USE OF ALCOHOL, DRUGS, ETC.

Whether the problem is alcohol, drugs, gambling, or anything else, it leads to behavior that makes a person unreliable and untrustworthy. It will inevitably prevent the addict from putting the partner's needs first. Feeding the addiction will always come first, not the partner.

71

- Does anyone in my partner's family have a history of addiction?
- Does my partner's drinking/drug use/gambling make me uncomfortable?
- Does he or she acknowledge that there is an addiction problem?
- Is he or she now in treatment or seeking professional help to overcome this addiction?

2. CONTROLLING OR BULLYING TENDENCIES

If you feel as if your partner tries to micromanage every detail of your relationship and your life, neither of you will feel as if you have a relationship of two independent, mature adults. If he insists on having his own way more than you think is fair or she does not respect your independence, then it won't be long before the two of you will experience conflict.

- Does he or she expect me to account for my whereabouts every single minute of the day? If I don't, does he or she express annoyance or worse?
- Does he or she constantly tell me what to do?
- Is he or she overly jealous and mistrustful when I spend any time away from him or her, or when I have any dealings with the opposite sex?
- Does he or she try to bully me into doing things I do not want to do?
- Does your partner fail to consult you on important decisions?

3. DISHONESTY AND LYING

The good relationships are built on trust. Each partner has to be able to rely on the other telling him or her the truth.

- Does my partner ever lie to me?
- Does my partner try to excuse his or her lying, rather than apologize for it?

4. DISPLAYS OF CONTEMPT, CONDESCENSION, AND OVERALL LACK OF RESPECT

If your partner treats you with contempt rather than respect and speaks sarcastically and condescendingly, it will be almost impossible to talk over your differences calmly and rationally.

- Does my partner make fun of me in a way that hurts my feelings?
- Does my partner make snide remarks about me and act as if he or she does not respect my skills, talents, or contributions?
- Do I feel that my partner does not treat me with respect?

5. EMOTIONAL WITHDRAWAL

If your partner has great trouble sharing his or her emotions or demonstrating love through affection and touch, in a way that meets your own emotional needs, it will be difficult to have a mutually satisfying relationship.

- Does my partner simply walk away or retreat when there is conflict rather than sit down to talk it through?
- Does my partner have difficulty expressing his or her feelings and emotions?
- Does my partner give the warmth, physical affection, and emotional nurturance I need, or does he or she seem to withhold emotional support?

6. EXCESSIVE OR EXPLOSIVE ANGER

When your partner's anger seems excessive, inappropriate to the circumstances, or occurs more often than you are comfortable with, he or she may have a problem.

- Does my partner shout excessively when there is even a slight disagreement?
- Does my partner's anger seem out of control or frightening to me?
- Have friends or family mentioned these outbursts to me?
- Is such behavior common in my partner's family?

7. EXTREME DEFENSIVENESS OR DENIAL THAT OBSTRUCTS OPEN DISCUSSION

If you try to bring up problems that you see in your interactions, and your partner seems unable to listen and instead gets angry, defensive, or completely denies your feelings, it will be difficult for you both to grow in this relationship. It also makes it difficult or impossible to fix problems as they arise.

- Does my partner jump on me or refuse to calmly discuss any differences of opinion that I bring up?
- Can my partner listen to problems I bring up, or does he or she usually deny that any such problems exist?

8. FREQUENT CRITICAL OR INSULTING REMARKS

Excessive criticism between partners is one of the most destructive behaviors in any relationship, and one most likely to lead to divorce.

If your partner repeatedly criticizes and insults you, he or she is not showing you the respect any marriage partner deserves.

- Does my partner show lack of respect in the way he or she talks to me?
- Does he or she repeatedly criticize who I am or what I do?
- Does he or she criticize me or insult me in front of others?

9. INFIDELITY

Unfaithfulness is one of the most fundamental betrayals of trust, and one that will jeopardize a marriage. If your partner is unfaithful before you get married, and you cannot agree that both of you find such actions unacceptable, chances are it will happen again.

- Does my partner flirt or behave in any other way with others that makes me unhappy or uncomfortable?
- Has my partner ever been unfaithful to me?
- Has my partner ever given me reason to believe he or she might be unfaithful?

10. INTOLERANCE OR EXCESSIVE RIGIDITY

Someone who is intolerant of you or others, or who is excessively rigid, will not be likely to have the forgiving nature or the flexibility and resilience to roll with the ups and downs that any long-term relationship requires.

- Is he or she accepting of attitudes I possess that differ from his or her own?
- Is he or she tolerant of me or my friends and relatives when they express views or behave in ways that may differ from his or her own?
- Does he or she get impatient or angry when people do not seem to agree with him or her?
- Does my partner refuse to speak to me or others if he or she is angry?

11. LAZINESS AND UNWILLINGNESS TO DO HIS OR HER SHARE

Once two partners agree on what they find to be a fair distribution of chores around the house, based on time and preferences and skills, it is not acceptable for one of the partners to repeatedly slack off without discussing it thoroughly with the other.

- Does my partner constantly avoid doing what he or she agreed to do or should do?
- Does my partner think household chores are always someone else's job, not his or hers?
- Does my partner refuse to pitch in and leave the lion's share of the work to me, even though we agreed to split things equitably?

12. RUDENESS OR BAD MANNERS

If your partner is repeatedly rude to you or others, or if his or her bad manners make you feel as if you would not want to be seen in public with him or her, your relationship cannot possibly become great without some major alterations in behavior.

- Am I embarrassed by my partner's manners?
- When I ask my partner to modify his or her behavior, is he or she able to change, or does the behavior persist?
- Does my partner seem rude in a way that I feel shows lack of respect for me and others?

13. SELFISHNESS OR INABILITY TO SHOW KINDNESS, CARING, AND SUPPORT

Be careful if your partner puts his or her interests above yours on a fairly regular basis. Such behavior is likely to encourage you to behave in a similar fashion, if only to protect your interests. When two people behave selfishly, they will likely grow farther apart over time.

- Do I feel as if my partner is pulling his or her share in the relationship?
- Am I happy about how chores and responsibilities are divided?
- Does my partner think about what I want and need as much as his or her own interests?
- Is my partner willing to help others when they need it?

14. VIOLENCE OR VERBAL ABUSE

Physical violence and verbal abuse are *never* acceptable in any relationship. With counseling, some individuals may be able to overcome this behavior. But if the person is unwilling to seek outside counseling, you shouldn't expect to see significant change.

- Does my partner use abusive language, profanity, or cruel and insulting remarks directed at me that I find offensive and hurtful?
- Has my partner ever hit me or threatened to hurt me—even once?

Though psychological and emotional problems may not be fatal flaws, they are conditions you must be aware of before you marry. If your partner is suffering from conditions such as depression, anxiety, obsessive fears, or other worrisome emotional issues, he or she should receive professional help before you make any decision about marrying. Of course, he or she should continue with that help, if necessary, after the marriage, should you decide to go ahead with it.

It can be very difficult to look honestly at the person we think we love. We may feel we'll spoil the romance, or discover things we wish we didn't know. But the reverse is more likely to be true. Having honest discussions—many of them—about religion, money, sex, children, recreation, and acceptable behavior can be a great way to discover how much you really have in common. It will also build trust and a strong foundation for your future life together. If you don't agree at first, this discussion offers a chance to learn what you need to continue working on. If you still aren't able to agree on all of these six basic issues, you will find it much wiser and less painful in the long run to part ways so that you can begin, with optimism, your new search for the *right* person for you.

CHAPTER FIVE

Decide about Marriage: Propose, Get Engaged, Make Your Wedding Meaningful

How do I love thee, let me count the ways.

—Elizabeth Barrett Browning

ECIDING ABOUT MARRIAGE IS EXCITING BUT NOT always easy. As your relationship becomes more serious and the two of you start having more frequent conversations about your future together, don't be surprised if you're feeling not only joy but occasionally also stress, and sometimes doubt. Even if you both are very much in love, even if you seem to have more in common with your partner than anyone you've ever been with before, you may still wonder whether this relationship will make you both happy forever.

It may be the first time you've felt so much in love with anyone, but you may still have doubts because it all seems so new. Or you may have been in serious long-term relationships before—or even married—and you may feel overwhelmed with the anxiety of "getting it right" this time.

Now is a good time to look at all the wonderful aspects of your relationship, as well as each of your concerns. You are about to make the most important decision of your life. Are you both ready to commit yourselves to each other for a lifetime? Do you really love each other so much that you want to spend the rest of your lives together?

The questions in the box on page 81 are designed to help you both decide with confidence whether this is it.

Deal with Lingering Doubts—Now

To have a great marriage, you should have very few doubts about your future together. If you are able to answer Yes to the questions in the box on page 81 and you feel confident that you have met your match, this would be the time to discuss your future with the person you love.

But if you have lingering doubts and concerns, do not be discouraged. You still have three options, and each one can have a silver lining.

YOU CAN CONTINUE DATING AND WORK ON RESOLVING THE PROBLEMS

Talk about your concerns with your partner. It can also be helpful to discuss your doubts with a parent, a close relative, a friend, or a professional counselor. Pay attention to their observations. If you don't feel comfortable discussing these worries now, they will likely only grow larger rather than disappear.

If you have serious doubts and get married anyway, the odds are that you'll be sorry. Don't let your desire to get married overpower those doubts. Continue seeing each other exclusively, but make a concerted effort to build a wonderful relationship with each other. Take another look at Chapter Three, "Put Love and Respect First" (p.47), to see ways you can deepen your bonds. The more helpful and loving you are, the better your relationship will become. Take walks together; talk, and listen to each other carefully; explore your sexual intimacy; spend more time with each other's friends and family—all the steps that we discuss in Part Three. Connecting in these ways will bring you closer together and clarify your strengths as a couple. It will also bring to light the areas you may need to work on to get yourselves ready for marriage.

WILL YOU HAVE A GREAT MARRIAGE?

Trust and honesty, coupled with love and respect, create the foundation for a strong, lasting relationship. Talk about your love for each other and any reservations you might have. Ask yourselves and each other these questions.

Are you both happy when you're together and feel that you have each other's best interests at heart? _____

Would you rather be with this person than with anyone else you've ever met? _____

Do you respect and admire your partner and feel you want to live with him or her, as he or she is, without expecting any significant changes? _____

Do you feel you know how to make your partner happy? Do you feel your partner knows how to make you happy? _____

Are you both committed to be faithful to each other for life? _____

Have you talked through the "Big Six" and are you comfortable that you have reached full agreement regarding religion, money, sex, children, recreation, and acceptable behavior? _____

Are you able to resolve your disagreements amicably, quickly, and in a way that satisfies you both? _____

Have you resolved any issues between you that you may have avoided discussing in the past? _____

Are you confident that despite your partner's flaws, you can accept him or her without feeling you are compromising? _____

Can you imagine yourselves living together as a happy couple twenty years from now? Fifty? _____

YOU CAN DECIDE TO PART WAYS, AT LEAST TEMPORARILY

Many couples who now have wonderful marriages previously decided to split up for a while, and then got back together months or years later. In some cases, one or both of them simply did not feel ready to make a decision that would commit them for the rest of their lives. They needed time apart, even time with other people, to see how they really felt.

Jeffrey and Elizabeth met in college and fell in love in their twenties. They stayed together a year after college graduation, but they both felt they were just too young to get married. They hadn't had enough experience to be absolutely sure this relationship was for life. They broke up, moved to different parts of the world, and dated other people for three years.

During all those years, wherever Jeffrey was, he kept his favorite picture of Elizabeth on his wall. No matter who Elizabeth dated, she kept the memory of Jeffrey in her mind. When they got back together three years later, they knew they were ready to marry each other and spend the rest of their lives together.

YOU CAN SPLIT NOW AND MAKE A FRESH START WITH SOMEONE NEW

Breaking up is hard to do. But if you part and decide not to reunite, at least you will be better prepared next time to find the right person for you.

All valuable relationships take work and time. Starting your search all over for the right person may seem daunting now, but staying with the wrong person would be much more difficult. Take another look at Chapter Two, "Date with Purpose" (p. 25). You'll find dozens of fun and practical ideas about how to find the person with whom you can be happy for the rest of your life. You'll be glad you did.

If Everything Feels Right, Go On—Propose

If you are ready to make a lifelong commitment to each other, there's still one more step to get both of you off to a great marriage. One of you has to take the leap and say the words that make the decision clear. One of you has to "pop the question." It can be a big moment or a quiet one, but it will always be one you'll remember.

Erin and Jamie will never forget the night seven years ago when Jamie proposed.

"We had been living together in this tiny apartment in Brooklyn for about three months and I came home from a terrible guitar lesson in a terrible mood," recalls Erin. "Taped to the door was a note: 'Erin, follow the flowers.' I opened the door and there was a line of roses on the floor leading all the way to the back of the apartment. It was like a florist's shop in the apartment. So I followed the roses and there was Jamie, down on one knee, holding out a ring box. He said, 'Erin, will you marry me?'"

"She was so excited about the proposal," Jamie continues, "that she didn't even notice for quite some time that the ring I gave her was plastic. I got a theatrical fake ring at a prop shop that looked like a 50-carat diamond because I wanted us to pick out the real ring together. But she didn't even notice it for hours. She was so happy, and I was happy and relieved, too. I was 99.9 percent sure she would accept, but there's always this question in your mind, 'What if she's not ready yet?' We just hugged and talked all night."

Other proposals may not be quite as elaborate but are still sweet to remember. Like the story of how two people meet, the story of the wedding proposal becomes a part of the fabric of your marriage together.

Gavin and Naomi met twenty-three years ago when Naomi, a human resources director, recruited him for a job at her company in New York. It was a publishing company that owned a number of magazines, including one for brides.

"After we dated awhile and I knew I wanted to marry her, I tried to think of an unusual way to ask her," says Gavin. "So I took the brides magazine, cut a square out of the middle of it, stuck the engagement ring in the square, and wrapped it up as a gift.

"When she took off the wrapping paper, she looked at the magazine and said, 'Why do I need this—I get it at the office?' I said, 'Open it.' When she found the engagement ring, she was excited and happy."

Proposals that happen spontaneously can be equally memorable. Sometimes, in the midst of doing something together that you both love—as simple as a hike—you come to see that what you share is strong enough to last forever.

Paul and Nancy had been dating for several years and had had an on-again, off-again kind of romance. After hiking to the top of a mountain one day, they sat looking at the magnificent view, and both said how wonderful it was being together. "Well, if it's so great," said Paul, "how come you never asked me to marry you?" Nancy replied, "How come you never asked me?" Nancy paused for a moment. "You're right," she said. "Will you marry me?" Paul just leaned over, kissed her tenderly on the lips, and said, "Of course—when do you want to do it?" Now, twelve years later, when they tell this story to their three children, the only thing they wonder is what took them so long to decide.

Use Your Engagement Period Wisely

Whether you decide to keep your engagement to yourselves or announce it to the world, you deserve to celebrate. A quiet dinner can be as special as a big party. The important thing to remember is that you are embarking on a new stage in your life which you hope will be filled with happiness. If you use this engagement period well, it will bring you closer to a great marriage.

The engagement period is a time to practice the loving behavior that will make your marriage successful. It should go without saying that you will continue to be faithful to each other—as you will throughout the rest of your lives. You will get to know each other better—and get acquainted with each other's families. This should also be the time to set the date to make your commitment public in a wedding ceremony.

Last Chance to Reconsider

Planning a wedding can be very stressful. "Wedding jitters" can strike even the happiest couples. Any change, even a positive one, takes some adjustment.

But you need to make sure you are just nervous about the wedding and not whether you have chosen the right person to marry. Don't let the momentum of party planning sweep you along. You must have the courage to work through differences or, if you cannot, to break off the engagement or even call off the wedding—no matter how far you have progressed with the preparations. However hard or embarrassing it might seem at the time, it is nothing compared to the pain of marrying the wrong person.

Many people who are now in great marriages broke off a previous engagement—even though the invitations had been sent out and the caterer was booked. They went on to brand-new relationships where they did not experience the hesitation and the doubts—and they ended up in very happy marriages.

Keep Your Wedding Plans Centered and Simple

Unless you plan to elope secretly in the dark of night, or have planned a small intimate wedding, you may soon find your wedding plans escalating out of control. This one-sentence wedding mantra may be helpful. Recite it to yourselves in those moments when everyone about you seems to be going crazy with the planning details: *The point of the wedding is to celebrate our love and make a public commitment to each other for life.*

Everything else is extra.

No matter what happens, your wedding is just the beginning.

The idea behind a formal wedding is to celebrate that you have found each other and want to stay together for the rest of your lives. The size of the wedding has nothing to do with whether or not you will have a great marriage. Neither does the quality of the food or the band or the bride's dress, or all of those hundreds of details that many couples spend endless months agonizing over. Make your wedding a celebration that brings you and your partner—and the family and friends who celebrate with you—closer together.

Resist outside pressure. Understand what you really want in the way of a wedding—talk calmly about the dreams you both have. Do you want a big wedding or is it your parents who want it? Could you be just as happy with a more intimate gathering? If you want something modest and your parents want something grander, see if you can work out a compromise that makes everyone happy. Your parents may want to invite some of their friends and family, and you will want to make them happy. But when it comes to your own guest list, ask yourselves if they are people you will want to see at your twenty-fifth wedding anniversary, too. If they're not really that close to you, why do you feel you must invite them now? You might consider saving some of the money you or your parents were thinking about spending on the wedding and devoting it to a great honeymoon or your first anniversary party or a down payment on a home, instead.

Your wedding day is just that—one day—out of more than 18,000 days you will have shared by your fiftieth anniversary. Twenty-four hours that should be memorable but do not have to be "perfect." No matter what happens, your wedding is just the beginning.

Focus on What's Important—Your Vows, Your Honeymoon, Your Commitment

To keep your wedding enjoyable and expressive without becoming stressful and perilously expensive, all you have to do is devote at least as much time to considering and writing your vows as you do to selecting the style of the invitations and the food the caterer will serve.

Remember, the wedding ceremony is more than a celebration. It is both a public commitment and a private contract. The bride and groom declare their love and articulate their promise and their commitment to enter into a union for a lifetime. It is usually witnessed by friends and family and the community, often blessed by a religious or spiritual leader, and recorded and sanctioned by the state.

The vows are your promises to each other to love, honor, cherish, and stand by each other, in sickness and in health, for as long as you both shall live. Whatever vows you decide to utter in your ceremony—and the choice is up to you—they will set the tone for your marriage. Your marriage will be built on how well you carry out those promises you make to each other. Those promises deserve your time and attention. Make them a celebration of what is special in your relationship and what qualities you want your marriage to uphold. You will think back on them often through your life together.

AVOID THESE COMMON WEDDING MISTAKES

It is very easy to get carried away as you plan for this landmark event and lose sight of your true aim: launching a great marriage. Here are common wedding mistakes you might want to watch out for...and avoid:

- **Spending too much money:** Many couples spend more money than they can comfortably afford, sometimes putting a serious financial and emotional strain on their new marriage.

  The average 150-to-200-guest wedding costs from $14,000–$30,000. The average cost is about $22,000, a sum that is equivalent to about twenty-two weeks of the median family income in 2002—or the down payment on a house.

- **Going into debt for the wedding:** Weddings are more expensive than ever. In addition, more and more couples are marrying later in life than a few decades ago and paying for their wedding themselves. Many couples feel established enough in their work lives to get exactly the wedding they want—and to pay for it themselves. Many are going into deep debt to do it. For couples under the age of thirty, debt from their wedding is the most common and intense source of conflict, according to a Creighton University study. Among couples of all ages surveyed, wedding debt was the third most troubling issue in their marriage, behind time management and sexual issues.

  To avoid these common wedding mistakes, keep the wedding meaningful and manageable. Set aside some of the money you save for a great honeymoon or maybe a house or a baby. And don't forget—enjoy the day.

Your honeymoon is important, too. It is more than just a special vacation. It is your chance to build up unique lifetime memories.

Along with your vows, writes Susan Page in *The Eight Essential Traits of Couples Who Thrive*, "a couple's honeymoon experience is a part of the distinctive shared history that makes them a couple. No one else was there. No one but the two of them knows exactly what it felt like. The heightened passion that they felt is something they can continue to draw upon throughout their lives for inspiration, motivation, and renewed love."

To keep your wedding enjoyable and expressive, devote at least as much time to considering and writing your vows as you do to selecting the style of the invitations and the food the caterer will serve.

Have Fun as Partners and Lovers

Remember, the real wedding between two partners does not take place in the hotel ballroom or the church or the synagogue. It takes place in your hearts and minds, in that moment when you make the commitment to be partners and lovers for life. And it takes place again and again as you renew that commitment to each other, each day, in the way you choose to love, honor, and cherish each other "from that day forth, as long as you both shall live."

PART THREE

Building a Joyful Life Together

CHAPTER SIX

Communicate Lovingly: Resolve Anger Quickly

I like not only to be loved, but to be told I am loved;
the realm of silence is large enough beyond the grave.

—GEORGE ELIOT

THE WAY COUPLES TALK TO EACH OTHER and treat each other in small ways, every day, sets the tone for their life together. A warm voice and a caring touch can make all the difference. Loving words and thoughtful action reflect the respect and love partners feel for each other. Sharing what's going on in your life with your partner allows you to understand each other and build a strong foundation of love.

You might think good communication between two people who love each other and who are committed to spending their lives together would flow naturally, like a gentle river moving from the source to the sea. But simply opening your mouth and speaking your mind may not always work the way you hoped. Communicating clearly and honestly involves skills and habits that you need to learn and practice. It also requires that you pay attention just as much to what you say with your body as with your words. Body language, facial expressions, and, most important, our attitudes contribute as much to communicating our thoughts and feelings as the sentences we speak.

Learning how to deal with anger quickly and kindly is also an essential part of loving communication between lifelong partners. It brings many rewards. You will not only make your home together a peaceful place, but you will build trust and deepen the bond between you.

View anger as a useful warning sign—a sign that somebody's needs or wants aren't being met, that we are feeling hurt, or that something is not right. A great marriage provides a safe place for both partners to express and resolve their differences and anger.

Even in a great relationship, there is no way to avoid occasional moments of anger and conflict. When two mature individuals feel deeply about each other—and about issues—there are bound to be occasional differences and disagreements.

The solution is not to avoid conflict. It is to resolve it as quickly and calmly as possible. *Couples who avoid arguments are more likely to get divorced than couples who are able to confront their differences and resolve them peacefully.* Instead, view anger as a useful warning sign—not that there is trouble in the relationship, but simply that there is a rough patch that needs attention. It is a sign that somebody's needs or wants aren't being met, that we are feeling hurt, or that something is not right. A great marriage provides a safe place for both partners to express and resolve their differences and anger.

"A certain amount of conflict is necessary to help couples weed out actions and ways of dealing with each other that can harm the marriage in the long run," says John Gottman, professor of psychology at the University of Washington and cofounder of the Seattle Marital and Family Institute. Occasional conflicts provide opportunities for couples to better understand each other's deepest likes, dislikes, concerns, and beliefs. Happily married couples learn to settle their disagreements—or come to an acceptance about their differences—quickly and lovingly. When that pattern becomes a habit, their relationship becomes stronger and even more satisfying.

"At times we get angry or upset," Gerry says. "But from the very beginning we decided we didn't want to go to bed angry. Lilo and I both know how important it is to say something nice to each other often—simple things like, 'I think you handled the kids' fight in the backseat of the car just right,' or 'I am so sorry I was late—I was really trying to get here early.' And we seldom go to sleep without kissing each other good night."

Communicating with Care

JUST LISTEN

Few activities convey how much you love and appreciate your partner as much as actively listening. Partners in happy marriages say they not only feel they can speak their mind, they feel their partner can truly *hear* what they are saying. Many arguments stem from one or both partners feeling as if they have not been heard. Don't interrupt each other. The happiest couples don't let much time pass without finding out how their lover and soul mate is doing. They want to know what their partner is thinking, as he or she wakes up, goes through the day, and slips under the covers at night.

The best way to begin actively listening to your partner is to try to put yourself into your partner's shoes. As your partner talks, try to listen to the tone as well as the words, imagine yourself in exactly your partner's situation, and try to feel exactly as he or she does. Don't say to yourself, "I wouldn't feel that way" or "I know how to fix this." Don't judge and don't "fix" anything. Just listen. Try to experience those same emotions. If your partner is hurt by something you said, imagine yourself feeling hurt by that same thing. Try not to get defensive. If you put yourself in your partner's place, you remove the obstacles to understanding.

One of the best ways to show your partner that you are listening is to ask questions and say, "Tell me more." It lets your partner know that you are paying close attention and that you care. It is also the best way to ensure that you do understand. Many of us assume we know our partner so well that we can figure out what is on his or her mind. But failing to draw our partner out to discover what is going on below the surface often leads to misunderstandings.

There's an easy technique you can use to let your partner know you have understood: Restate what your partner just said, in slightly different form, and make sure it matches what your partner was trying to communicate. For example, you might say, "I see, so when I don't get home for dinner, even though I said I would, you feel as if I don't care about you enough to take the time to be there, is that right?" Don't jump in to defend yourself or respond. Just understand. Then you both will be ready to come up with a fair solution. "I am sorry. I didn't know it meant that much to you, and I certainly didn't think you'd interpret it as my not caring. I do care. Let's try again tomorrow, and this time I'll be early."

Angela says her husband Tim shows how much he cares in his "typically calm way." He listens.

"He always listened to what I had to say and I liked that," Angela says. "I came from a family where everybody was always yelling or talking. It was a big Italian family. So it was nice to have someone who listened, and who was interested in what I was doing and what I thought about things. He was different from the other boys I had dated… Now, thirty-six years later, he's still a good listener."

SPEAK LOVINGLY AND WITH RESPECT

All of us need to feel loved, appreciated, and respected. No matter how confident we may appear, we all have sensitive egos that can be deeply hurt by harsh words. We need to experience our partner's positive regard on a regular basis, not just on special occasions or when we've done something out of the ordinary.

Happy couples routinely compliment each other. They let each other know how much they enjoy being together and having each other in their lives. Expressing appreciation builds trust and good will. It also makes it more likely that your partner will remember to reciprocate with a loving comment—so the good feelings keep building.

Expressing appreciation builds trust and good will.

Communicating respectfully also extends to how you treat each other in public. It is important to act in ways that make your spouse comfortable. Birthdays and anniversaries are common occasions when misunderstandings can arise. Some people like to have a big public fuss made over their birthday—it makes them feel as if their partner thinks they are special. Others find surprise parties or even birthday cakes with candles at restaurants acutely embarrassing and uncomfortable. Consider how your partner feels—and honor that, even if he or she feels differently from you.

Larry, happily married to Cindy for twenty-three years, remembers the first few years of their marriage, when he rarely told her he loved her. "When she first brought it up, I said, 'I told you I loved you when we got married. Nothing has changed. If it had changed, I would have let you know.' I'm an engineer—we try to keep things simple."

Cindy was able to laugh about it because she knew he didn't mean to be flippant or ungrateful—that was just how his mind worked. But with a little gentle guidance by example from her, Larry learned to let her know more often how much he cared, even if his feelings hadn't changed.

WHAT IS YOUR COMMUNICATION STYLE?

Individuals have unique styles of communication. Some people are fast talkers, others slower. Some are forceful and dramatic, others understated and quiet. If you and your partner understand that there is no right or wrong style, you can appreciate your differences and accommodate them.

Try to find a middle ground. The fast talker should learn to refrain from finishing the other's sentences. The slower talker should not feel as if he or she has to speed up to keep the other partner interested. Each should try to remember why they found their partner's differences attractive when they first met. The fast talker seemed witty and charming. The slow talker seemed relaxed, deliberate, and easygoing. Let your different approaches smooth each other's rough edges and allow you both to communicate on a deeper level. As Dave Meurer wrote in his humorous book, *Daze of Our Wives: A Semi-Helpful Guide to Marital Bliss*, "A great marriage is not when the 'perfect couple' comes together. It is when an imperfect couple learns to enjoy their differences."

Men and women do seem to display different characteristic tendencies in communication. Researchers like Deborah Tannen have observed that one of the most significant of these gender differences is that men tend to use conversation to solve problems while women tend to use conversation to express feelings, connect with another person, and establish rapport.

For example, a woman might come home from work and say to her husband, "You wouldn't believe what my boss said to me today. He is such a jerk." Her husband, instead of simply listening to her tale, might jump in with, "Why don't you get a new job or quit?" She wanted him to simply listen and sympathize. He felt he had to be helpful by coming up with a solution to the problem. She gets mad because she thinks he doesn't really care enough to listen to her situation. He is totally confused by her anger because he just wanted to offer concrete help.

They both were doing what they do best. She was sharing her feelings; he was solving her problem. But they misunderstood each other's needs and motives. What could have been a moment of closeness turned into an argument.

Couples need to recognize that just because they each may have a male or female conversational style, they can still learn how to adapt to the other's way of talking. Both have to listen and understand what is important to the other person.

If she had let him know, right at the beginning of the conversation, that she just wanted to talk about her feelings, get her problems off her chest, without coming up with a solution, then he might have known what she needed and he could have relaxed and listened.

If he just listened and sympathized first, she probably would have been more receptive to his asking, a little later on, if she wanted to think about possible solutions. That way, each honors the other's approach, and they both get what they need.

ASK FOR WHAT YOU WANT—ESPECIALLY IF WHAT YOU WANT CHANGES OVER TIME

It couldn't sound simpler, but people often hesitate to say what they really want. There are many reasons. They may not know what they want. Or they may fear their partner will deny their request, leaving them feeling rejected and unloved. Or they may feel embarrassed and worried that their request may sound silly or selfish. Often it can seem like it's never the right time. We may feel that asking for what we want spoils the joy of getting it—our partner should just magically know without our asking.

Happy partners realize they each have to figure out what they really want, be specific in explaining it, and ask for it clearly. It is important to begin the request by letting your partner know that you are not criticizing the way things went on before. "I really love the way we make love and am very happy with our lovemaking. I was just wondering if we might try this one new thing." That prevents your partner from responding defensively and enables him or her to consider your request calmly. It also increases the chances your partner will say "Yes" to your request, which can make you both happier.

When you change your feelings about what you want or need, don't keep your partner in the dark. For example, you may have established a rule at the beginning of your relationship not to exchange anything but "gag" birthday presents because you thought it was fun or money was very tight. But maybe now, after several years together, you may feel as if you'd like to surprise your partner with something more serious and romantic on his or her birthday. It is vital to keep talking and let your partner know your feelings have changed. Don't expect your partner to read your mind.

AVOID CRITICISM, BLAME AND SILENCE

Criticism can become a major obstacle to a loving relationship. Avoid accusations that begin, "You always" or "You never." They are destructive. You are much more likely to get your partner to understand what you want with positive statements rather than negative ones.

If your partner says or does something that bothers you, don't be critical. Try talking about how you feel. "I feel hurt when you . . ." or "I feel better when you . . ." It allows your partner to hear your concern without getting defensive. It sets a caring tone that produces the best atmosphere for a great partnership. If you find your voices rising, stop, take a break, and think about how much you really love each other. That is why you are bothering to discuss your problems in the first place.

Don't try to change the subject or interrupt before your partner is done. He or she will think you don't care.

Be honest, but don't forget to be sensitive and diplomatic, too. The happiest couples say they take care not to utter everything that crosses their mind without thinking first if it might hurt their partner. They also try to focus on the positive things to say to each other, rather than the negative.

"We have no secrets," says Nick, a computer specialist who has been happily married to Linda for nine years, "but I think a person who is stream-of-consciousness truthful, who says whatever is on his or her mind without editing, is an ass. Tact is very important."

Whatever you do, do not give up on communicating. *Both* partners have to understand that "the silent treatment" can only lead to disaster. Keep talking to each other—with patience and love. Every time you are caring and thoughtful, you are making a choice to enrich and stabilize your relationship. Silence, on the other hand, can sometimes be worse than angry words. It encourages "mind reading," which—as anyone who has ever tried it knows—more often than not leads to further misunderstandings.

Keep talking to each other—with patience and love. Every time you are caring and thoughtful, you are making a choice to enrich and stabilize your relationship.

Body Language Counts

Body language, too, can send a message as loud as your words—and it may not be sending the message you had in mind. For example, if you tend to cross your arms over your chest as you stand or sit, you may view this as a simple habit. But to others it looks like you are shielding yourself from your partner and it makes you appear aloof and defensive. It sends the message that you are not really opening up to listening to your partner.

Facial expressions matter, too. If you are looking out the window or across the room instead of making eye contact directly with your partner, again you are giving the impression of being bored, distracted, or, even worse, dishonest and unable to meet your partner's gaze openly. Rolling your eyes is even worse. This simple expression conveys impatience at best and contempt at worst. Both signals are likely to increase tension and hostility, not bring you closer.

Handle Anger with Care

RESOLVE DISPUTES QUICKLY

The happiest partners try not to let disagreements escalate into angry outbursts. They let each other know when they are not happy and deal with their problems openly, avoiding defensiveness, accusations, and acrimony. As Ann Landers once said in her newspaper advice column: "All married couples should learn the art of battle as they should learn the art of making love. Good battle is objective and honest—never vicious or cruel. Good battle is healthy and constructive, and brings to a marriage the principle of equal partnership."

GET TO THE ROOT OF THE ANGER

Don't jump to the conclusion that your spouse is deliberately trying to hurt or provoke you. Just state your differences plainly. Do not bring up old arguments or tangential grievances—when people get mad, they can be tempted to throw in every complaint they can think of. Stick to the subject at hand.

Understand that your partner's anger means that you have probably touched a nerve in a sensitive area that he or she cares about deeply. Resist the temptation to get angry in return. If you are aggressive, rude, controlling, or negative, the anger will only escalate. If both of you get angry, you will never get to the bottom of what caused the anger. You won't be able to work toward a resolution.

If your partner is angry, your first job is to stay calm.

If you have to err on one side or the other, try to listen more than you speak. "We have two ears and only one tongue in order that we may hear more and speak less," said Diogenes. Chances are, you both will have equal time over the long haul.

Sometimes it is difficult to figure out why one of you is angry. Our experience tells us to start with the simplest explanation first.

"We learned to look for the simple problem the hard way," Becky recalls. "One Friday we got into such a huge argument over what movie to go to that we almost canceled the entire evening's plans. It didn't dawn on us until we sat down at the restaurant and devoured all the bread in the bread basket that we both had been famished. Once we had a little food in our stomachs, we agreed on a movie in no time."

"We still laugh when we remember that night," Alan adds. "For all these years now, we know when we start arguing around dinnertime that we need to take a break—and find a snack fast."

At the very beginning of your disagreement, stop for a moment to ask yourself—and your partner—if either of you might be hungry, unusually tired, overextended, in pain or under stress, off your schedule of medication, or anxious about health, work, or family issues.

Any of these situations can make a disagreement worse. Try to address these immediate concerns, even if temporarily. Have a snack, take a nap, or go for a walk before you proceed to look for the real issues that may be the source of your conflict.

DON'T USE ANGER TO GET ATTENTION

Even happily married partners sometimes feel so frustrated that they say getting angry is the only way they can get their partner's attention. But there are better ways.

Unless you can defuse the tension and anger and bring your tempers down, neither of you will be able to get at the truth of what is bothering you. And you will certainly not be able to come to a solution.

Anger creates distance between two people. If you suspect that your partner feels as if you don't care what he or she is upset about, take the time to let your partner know you have been listening. Even if you don't have a solution, paying attention to each other will bring you closer.

REMEMBER, NO ONE IS RIGHT OR WRONG

"Sometimes it's worse to win a fight than to lose," Billie Holiday once said. Your aim should be to work toward a resolution that makes you both happy. The aim is not for one of you to "win" to prove who's "right." Two people can disagree without either one having to be wrong, just as two people can come to an agreement without one or the other being right.

Donald, who has been married to Francine for thirteen years, says,

COULD YOU BE PROVOKING YOUR PARTNER'S ANGER?

Any number of things can trigger anger but there are certain behaviors that are more likely than others to cause trouble. See if any of these scenarios sound familiar.

- One of you is trying to control the situation, rather than understand it and your partner. Anger is often about feeling ignored and not heard.
- One of you is responding to the other's problem or complaint with impatience or rudeness, rather than trying to listen and understand. Anger can result when you feel as if you cannot fully express your feelings.
- One of you may be reacting to something you or your partner is characteristically doing or not doing, saying or not saying. This should be the time to start working on changing that troublesome, recurring behavior that upsets your partner.

"I think our marriage works successfully because we're both willing to invest the time in settling our differences peacefully. And neither of us is convinced that we're right all the time."

Whether the source of the anger turns out to be something you are doing or something your partner is doing, it takes both of you pitching in to help each other work toward a solution. The best resolution will often be different from what either one of you thought you wanted. Even if one partner is taking primary responsibility for changing a pattern or behavior that is causing anger, the other partner should offer continued support and be willing to make some changes, too.

Try to keep this in mind. *Only one of you can get angry at a time.* Even if your partner's behavior makes you angry, or you think that he or she is being unreasonable, don't react with anger. It may require real strength of character and ego to resist, but don't give in. Stay calm.

Remind yourselves that you love each other and that, no matter how serious this current issue may feel at the time, you both know you will endure together.

Joanne, who has been happily married for twenty-five years, says,

"We figured out pretty early that both people couldn't be angry at the same time. We came up with that rule after the toothbrush fight—at least that's what we call it. I was upstairs reading and Dean was down in the shop, woodworking. I went downstairs. I had my toothbrush in my mouth, and I said, 'Hey, you wanna come to bed?' And he said, 'Yeah, yeah, yeah, in a while.' So I went back upstairs, read my book for a while, and went back downstairs. 'Wanna come to bed?' He said, 'Yeah, in a while, I said I would.' And he started getting mad, too.

"Now I didn't want to go to bed, I wanted him to have sex with me, right? But I was too embarrassed to come right out and say that. I went up and down three flights of steps about eight times, and we were both getting really mad. I kept interrupting him; he kept ignoring me.

"Finally, I stood there with the toothbrush still in my mouth, waiting for him to look up, and I just said, 'Will you have sex with me?'

"Well, then he looked up. 'Oh, why didn't you just say that in the first place? I would have been right up!'"

FOCUS ON THE FUTURE, NOT THE PAST

Your aim is to come to a resolution that makes you both happy, now and in the future. To do this it helps to focus more on the future than the past. Do not drag up old wounds, old arguments. Once you both understand what is upsetting you, come up with a plan for making things happen differently in the future.

Brainstorm options that can satisfy you both. Reassure each other that even if you can't think up the perfect solution right now, you both will keep thinking about it.

In even the best marriages, sometimes there isn't a solution that can make you both equally happy. One partner may want the kids to go to parochial school, the other to public school; one may want to vacation in a warm spot where you can swim, the other wants the cold ski slopes. The solution might be to take turns on the vacation plans or perhaps do something new and different that you'll both enjoy. The important thing is to let each other know that you are confident you will eventually find a solution that will make you both happy now and for the rest of your lives.

SAYING "I'M SORRY" NEVER HURTS

Be willing to admit when you are wrong. And be willing to say you're sorry, whether you are wrong or not. Apologize when you have been unkind—even if you think your position was right. There's a difference. Being kind is more important to a good marriage than being right.

Being kind is more important to a good marriage than being right.

Not all ways of saying, "I'm sorry" are equal. Saying "I'm sorry you feel that way," just puts the blame for the problem back on your partner and doesn't show you have heard or understood at all—let alone that you are sorry for having played any part in the problem. Try instead: "I'm sorry I made you angry."

Or simply follow Ogden Nash's sound advice resolving conflicts peacefully:

To keep your marriage brimming
With love in the marriage cup,
Whenever you're wrong, admit it;
Whenever you're right, shut up.

TRY NOT TO FIGHT IN FRONT OF THE KIDS

It is best to keep parental disagreements out of earshot of the kids. Especially when they are young, they can find your disputes upsetting, confusing, and frightening.

But if you realize that the kids may have overheard, sit down with them and explain that even happily married couples sometimes have disagreements. Tell them it is perfectly normal and that you are both working together to solve your dispute. You provide the best role models when you show your children that adults don't hide their differences—they talk them over and come to an agreement—and go on loving each other as much as before.

Francine says she and Donald try to show the children that arguments can be settled calmly. "I grew up in a house with a lot of anger," Francine says. "So I really am trying to be more patient and more understanding and not go back to what I saw growing up. We both know that our children are really looking to us to be role models for so many things, but especially in our marriage. I cringe when I think of the times I have gotten really angry around the children. I don't want my sons to think blowing up is okay and then wind up losing their temper all the time or marrying someone who can't control her anger."

DON'T GO TO BED ANGRY

Even if you cannot solve every problem at one sitting, that does not mean you have to go to bed angry. You can agree to continue your discussion tomorrow, but you can also agree to let the anger go for the night. Even if you have only moved a step closer toward understanding each other and have not even begun to resolve the problem, congratulate each other on handling your disagreement maturely. Remind each other how lucky you are—even as you disagree—to have each other to disagree with.

Harry and Joyce try many tactics to keep from going to bed angry. "I try to use humor to defuse the situation," Joyce says. "Sometimes it's hard to laugh when you're angry. But it's also hard to be angry when you laugh." Harry adds, "I put the things I am angry about right on the table because I want to get it over with. I don't like being angry for more than a moment—or maybe a couple of hours at the most. But I never let it go on for days. We always try to make up before bedtime."

Regardless of what the day has done to you, kiss each other good night and resolve to continue tomorrow working toward a happy resolution together. It is critical not only to resolve anger but also to make your partner feel good about your life together every day.

"We never went to bed without saying 'I love you,'" begins Patrick. "And kissing each other good night," continues Louise. "If it was a good day, it was a big kiss. And if we had an argument, it might be a peck." Pat has the final word: "But we'd still end up with, 'I love you.'"

Best of all, to keep anger at a minimum in your relationship, try not to get angry in the first place. Show admiration for each other (see Chapter Three, "Put Love and Respect First" [p. 47]). Do what it takes to make your partner feel good about you, your life together, and your marriage every day.

CHAPTER SEVEN

Make Sex Great for Both of You: Deepen Your Bond

Soul meets soul on lovers' lips.

—PERCY BYSSHE SHELLEY

A GREAT MARRIAGE IS ONE IN WHICH YOU are both partners and lovers for life. Sex offers a powerful way to express your love and make your partner feel loved. It allows you to open up with each other and share intimacies that bring you closer than any other single thing you do as a couple. That's why the expression for *sex* is *making love*.

If you want a great marriage, you have to make the sex great—for both of you. Great sex depends upon a physical and emotional relationship that totally satisfies both partners and makes you both happy you are together. It is not just the icing on the cake; it is one of the most important ingredients in the cake. In *The Exceptional Seven Percent* Gregory Popcak writes, "It is as if, through lovemaking, the husband and wife say to each other, 'Look how well we love one another, even our bodies work for each other's good!'"

Partners in great marriages talk about their relationship as a lifelong courtship.

Sex is enhanced by daily demonstrations of affection between partners. With affection, unlike sex itself, frequency matters. More is better. Partners in great marriages talk about their relationship as a lifelong courtship. They go out of their way to touch and cuddle in the course of a day—as they say good-bye in the morning, as they pass each other in the hall, while they do the dishes—even when they know most of these touches will not culminate in sex. Many couples say that if the sex is good between them, everything else in their lives has a way of working itself out.

"The chemistry between Karen and me has always been great," Tom says. "Maybe it's because we just enjoy being with each other and are willing to do whatever it takes to keep things loving. About ten years ago, when we'd been married for more than forty years, we attended a weekend Tantric sex workshop, just for the fun of it. It added another dimension and made something that was already great even better."

With affection, unlike sex itself, frequency matters. More is better.

Happy Couples Make Time for Sex

The most important thing you can do to make sex great is to make time for it. No matter what. It may mean you get less sleep sometimes, or you have to skip lunch on a Saturday afternoon, but you'll discover that such "sacrifices" turn out not to be sacrifices at all.

Over the years, you'll find that many factors can have an influence on the quantity and quality of your sexual relations. Moods and hormones, the birth of children, your performance and your partner's, and the ups and downs of work and family life can all play a part. But one thing should never change: happy couples insist that, through it all, they make time for making love.

Sandra, married three times over the last fifty years, has a wise perspective on sex and marriage.

"I have been widowed twice and I'm now on my third loving relationship, so I have been through my fair share of good times and bad, love and anger and grief. But in all three of my marriages, I would have to say, when the sex is good, we seem able to handle all the other problems."

Practice Makes Perfect

Learn as much as you can about what pleases your partner and yourself. Read books on the subject, alone and together—it can be enjoyable as well as instructive. Put at least the same energy and devotion into learning how to make sex wonderful as you would put into learning how to improve your cooking skills or your guitar playing or anything else you regard as pleasurable and important in your life.

Learning about having good sex together means being willing to let each other know, openly, what really gives you pleasure and exploring new things that make you both feel great. If you're lucky, this learning process never ends. If you always make love in the dark, try it with the lights on or with some beautiful candles lit around the room. If you usually close your eyes when you kiss, try kissing with your eyes wide open. Try to reach each other intimately, with love, openness, and trust.

If you and your partner can talk together about your needs, wants, and desires, and can focus on what you both enjoy, your sex life will get better and better.

Jim and Cynthia, married fifty-two years, believe the secret to a happy marriage is to have sex often and to make it satisfying every time.

"Sex can be very different at different times." Jim explains. "It can be athletic or gentle, playful or passionate, exciting or calming, or combinations of all of those things, and can change over the years. But the one thing it always has to be is satisfying for both partners. As far as I'm concerned, if sex doesn't include an orgasm for both of us, one of us is being lazy or short-changed. End of story. You should be able to make your partner feel wonderful. When it's over, I feel as if I love Cynthia even more."

Good Sex Begins Outside the Bedroom: Touch Each Other Often

The path to great sex begins long before you both get into bed. It begins with small gestures: cooking dinner for your partner, the way you look at each other when you say good morning or good-bye, the way you touch when you sit next to each other, the way you think about each other throughout the day.

Some books call these kinds of interactions the real foreplay to sex. "Foreplay is everything that happened between you and your partner since the last time you had sex. How you treat each other with your clothes on has far more impact on what happens in bed than carefully planted kisses right before intercourse," according to *Guide to Getting It On: The Universe's Coolest and Most Informative Book About Sex*.

The goals of good sex are to make you feel warm, intimate, and closer together as well as to give you pleasure.

Francine, married to Donald for thirteen years, says their love is reflected in their sex life together.

"I would say sex is the barometer of how healthy our marriage is. As you grow together and the love gets deeper, the sex gets better and better. I never believed that could happen. But I am happy to report that it's true. Sex is the true expression of how you feel about each other."

Great sex depends on real emotional intimacy and connection. That comes about in many ways—touching each other lovingly plays a big part.

"I think the key to a good sex life is wanting to be touched," says Carol, as Ronald, her husband for over fifty years, takes hold of her hand. "Your skin has to want to be touched by his skin. Ours does." Ronald adds: "On a scale of one to ten, we'd rate our sex life an eleven!"

Intimacy Is a Lifestyle

Intimacy is more complicated than trying most of the body positions in the *Kama Sutra*—and far more satisfying. It depends on striving each day to reach out and do more than touch your partner—you need to really understand and pay attention to your partner, too.

That means being affectionate and being attentive to your partner's moods and needs—spoken and unspoken. Share your fantasies, experiment, but also respect each other's boundaries and sensitivities.

Intimacy is more complicated than trying most of the body positions in the *Kama Sutra*—and far more satisfying.

Josie, married twenty-five years to Jamie, say sex is always good, but sometimes it's even better than others.

"Sex with my husband is the best when we both can let go and just be ourselves," Josie says. "I can be the silliest person in the world— or the sexiest. I don't feel afraid to open up and enjoy whatever he does to me. And I feel free to try whatever pops into my head to please him and drive him wild. I don't have to worry about him judging me or what I am doing because I feel completely loved. It feels so good to be able to show him that I love him this way, too."

How Often Should You Make Love?

There is no simple answer to this question, no number that will guarantee a happy sex life. Some people want to engage in sex more frequently than others—and each of your needs may change from day to day or week to week. What is important is that you both discuss how you feel and make sure *both* of your needs and desires are being met.

It may take a little experimentation to establish a pattern that meets the needs of both of you. There is that scene in Woody Allen's movie *Annie Hall* where her therapist asks how often Annie has sex. Annie responds: "*Constantly*. Three times a week." When Alvie's therapist asks him the identical question, "How often?" Alvie responds to the same facts with the opposite feeling: "*Never*. Three times a week."

Though the cliché is that men want sex more frequently than women, the reality can go either way. If you want sex more often than your partner, you might try making your next sexual encounter so good for your spouse that he or she will be the one to start asking to do it more often.

The *real* issue is not so much "how often" but rather whether you both feel your needs are being satisfied. So don't be embarrassed to express your feelings—and keep the lines of communication open.

Gail and Steve, married fourteen years, have a built-in "couples clock" for when it's time to make love.

As Gail explains it, "When we start having little arguments over nothing and we snap at each other about dumb things like chores, I say to myself, 'Hmm, when was the last time we had sex? It must be about time.' And sure enough, once we do, we get along great again. We're *both* happy to take out the garbage."

Handle Problems As Soon As They Crop Up

Even good sex partners with strong sexual chemistry sometimes start feeling as if they are in a rut or not fully satisfied. The most important thing to do is talk. It may be difficult to bring such a sensitive subject out into the open, but your relationship will only get more awkward and distant if you avoid this central part of your life together.

Read books on sex together—and alone. (See "Recommended Reading" on page 181 for a list of some great books.) Talk about what each of you thinks of as a great sexual experience. Share your thoughts about some of the most wonderful times you've had making love to each other. When you are both in a calm, relaxed mood— but not in the middle of sex—discuss what you like and don't like as much, what other things you might like to try together. Once you can focus on your shared aim to please and satisfy the other, the rest will flow, if you keep in touch, verbally and physically.

If you have troubles that persist even after you have talked matters over together calmly and lovingly, seek outside help. A couples retreat or a talk with a sex counselor or marriage counselor can sometimes work wonders toward improving your relations. Good sex helps to keep everything else in your marriage running on track. When something goes wrong in that department, it's hard to keep your sense of perspective about the rest of your marriage.

Tim and Angela were pleasantly surprised to find that when they worked to improve how they related outside the bedroom, they felt big improvements in the bedroom as well.

"We were definitely in a rut a while back," says Tim. "But we didn't just change our sexual life—we started communicating better, laughing together, and we brought all that to the bedroom. We realized you're making love all the time, whether you're in the kitchen or driving in the car to the movies."

"It's a whole lot more fun now," Angela adds. "The gentleness and the thoughtfulness all play a part in the sex, like Tim calling me during the day just to say hello. Here's another thing we still do—and our kids make fun of us, but I know they love it. We leave little notes to each other, in the spot where we typically sit at the table, if Tim leaves before I do in the morning, or I leave before he does. Just little notes: 'I'll be thinking of you, I can't wait to come home, I love you.'"

"Yeah," Tim agrees, "the kids love that. I didn't realize that they loved it until they got married and they said, 'Whoa! I wonder if my husband's going to write a little note on my spot?'"

Reduce Stress—and Increase Desire

Chronic stress is not only bad for your health, it's bad for your sex life. Stress kills desire and passion. You need to feel safe, relaxed, and calm to really enjoy sexual relations with your partner for life.

Get enough sleep. Exercise regularly to release tension, raise your endorphin levels, and increase your energy. (See Chapter Ten, "Build a Happy, Healthy Life Together" on page 143.) Learn relaxation techniques. All these steps will also help you feel and look your best for your partner, which can only help increase the passion between you.

Harry believes staying fit is sexy.

"I've made it a point—and so has Joyce—to stay physically fit. Every day we try to go out for a walk, get some exercise and fresh air. That helps us keep in balance. And it keeps us in the mood, too, if you know what I mean."

Keep Expectations High

Sex can be just as good at eighty as it was at eighteen—different, maybe, but just as satisfying and exciting. Many couples even say it gets better the longer they are together. That's a challenge for both of you.

Rebecca and Bob, married fourteen years, say sex has only gotten better over the years. Rebecca is the first to say it: "Sex is very important to both of us. I guess you get better at it. As you grow and learn together and the love gets deeper, the sex gets better and better. It's the true expression of how you feel about each other."

"When you're younger there's a lot of lust involved so it all seems easy," Bob adds. "We make sure to keep that chemistry going by keeping in touch with each other's bodies, especially when we're naked. So many things can add to the pleasure of sex. It's as good as your imagination."

Try a Double Bed

It may be just a coincidence, but we have noticed that the rising curve in the rate of divorce in the Untited States over the last forty years is very similar to the curve that charts the growing use of king-sized beds versus double beds. Nobody has said that there is a cause-and-effect relationship, and lots of people with good marriages happily sleep in king-sized beds, but we do think that many people might find double beds preferable, once they have gotten used to them.

There are few things nicer than keeping in touch physically when you go to sleep, making you feel warm, cozy, and ready to snuggle up. We have interviewed people who have slept together in a double bed for their entire lives together, and they tell us they love the way they are almost touching. It is also a great recipe for putting you in the mood for love. They wouldn't change beds for anything, and it could work for you, too.

CHAPTER EIGHT

Share the Work
and Decision Making:
Find a Balance on Money,
Careers, and Chores

The more you invest in a marriage, the more valuable it becomes.

—AMY GRANT

IF YOU WANT TO HAVE A HAPPY life together, then joint decision making is a habit you need to set in place right from the beginning. When you decide on important issues together, you are showing respect for each other's opinions and wishes. Not only are you more likely to find solutions that will please you both, the process itself helps you to know each other better and trust each other more. It also can help you to come up with a better solution together than either of you might come up with alone.

Even though one of you may be more knowledgeable about, say, money matters, or one of you may take primary responsibility for household chores, or one of you may feel more strongly than the other about where you will live, or one of you earns more, or works more hours outside the home—none of that changes the basic rule. Both of you have to take part in deciding about matters that affect both of your lives, whether you are talking about which car to buy, whom to invite for dinner, where to hang a picture, how to invest, or starting a business.

"Karen and I would never think of making a big decision without discussing it—and 'big' doesn't have to mean it involves a lot of money," says Tom, who has been happily married for more than fifty years. "We talk over where we should hang paintings in the house or what color to paint a wall, too, because that affects what you look at every day of your lives. I ask myself, 'Would Karen want to be consulted about this?' She asks herself the same. If the answer is yes, we take the time to decide together. Sometimes it takes a little longer that way, but it's worth it. It's our way to show how much we love each other and care about making each other happy."

Establish Your Own Style of Decision Making

It's important to find a process for joint decision making that plays to each of your strengths. You may have to try a few patterns to hit upon a style that suits you both best.

Ask yourselves these questions:

- Do you like to have a sit-down discussion and go over all the details that will help you both make sound choices?
- Do you like one person to do most of the research and planning and then check in with the other for an okay?
- Do you like to come back to a topic several times, or do you prefer getting to a conclusion as quickly as possible?
- Do you feel more comfortable alternating which partner takes the lead in the lists and research for a major decision?

Over time you'll find a pattern that suits you as a couple and family.

The issues below are important to keep in mind as you establish your own decision making habits.

Behave As Equal Partners

Great marriage partners think of themselves as equals, each with something unique to contribute. They share major decisions and divide up others between them—otherwise they'd never get anything accomplished.

Bear in mind that wise choices often result from the clash of strong opinions. Not every decision will make both of you ecstatic. Sometimes you will just have to roll with things. Remember, few choices are actually life-threatening. It's *how* you make the choices that most affects the way you feel about each other. Make sure there is a balance of power between you so neither one of you feels as if you are always giving in to keep the peace.

Remember, few choices are actually life-threatening. It's *how* you make the choices that most affects the way you feel about each other.

Think About How Each Choice Affects You Both

Health problems, for example, may seem to affect only one partner, but the health implications of any significant medical choice affect both of you. You need to explore the options together and share the decision making about the best course of action to take.

On significant issues such as those involving the children, both parents need to take the time, out of hearing of the children, to come to a consensus. When you can present a united front as parents to the children, it strengthens the family and your marriage.

With extended family, even if it is a matter affecting only, say, *your* parents, include your partner in the decision. Both sets of parents will become both your responsibility. Try to come up with a solution that you can both feel good about.

Even in smaller decisions such as choices about furniture or placement of artwork in your house, which affect the environment you live or work in every day, it is important to consult each other and understand what pleases the other.

"Lilo and I still laugh about the incident of 'the ugly chair,'" Gerry says. "Lilo picked a fabric to reupholster a chair because she thought I would like it. She sent the fabric over to the office for me to look at. When I saw it, I wasn't crazy about it, but I thought she picked it because she liked it. So I said it was fine. When the chair came back, we both looked at it and said we hated it. She thought I would like it,

I thought she would like it. And neither of us liked it. The moral is, if you're not sure what will please your partner about something that touches your life every day, make the choice together," Gerry says.

In all of these areas that affect you both, you will enjoy an added advantage when you share your opinions. Not only do you each have a chance to voice your views, but you are more likely to come up with the best way of handling the situation—for both of you.

Trust Each Other to Act Independently

There are times when issues are of consequence to only one partner or one partner clearly has a greater stake in the decision and more expertise in making the choice. In those cases, it may be a better use of time and energy to give that partner the freedom to make the decision independently. Even when you decide on matters alone, think about making a decision that will please your partner, or at least will be acceptable. Let your partner know what decision you are considering and why, and listen to your partner's comments. Trust each other's choices—and tell your partner you do.

Don't surprise your partner by making a decision that affects both of you (or your children or the common space around the house) unless you are absolutely certain the decision will be welcomed.

You may discover that one of you is better at some tasks than others, such as paying bills, picking a good investment strategy, researching the best vacation spot or the most worthy charity to support. Even if one of you takes the lead, it is always better to talk it over before making the final purchase, decision, or expenditure.

When in doubt, err on the side of consulting your partner, rather than deciding something on your own and presenting it as a *fait accompli*. Don't surprise your partner by making a decision that affects both of you (or your children or the common space around the house) unless you are absolutely certain the decision will be welcomed. Sharing the process of deciding is part of the point—

each decision increases your comfort level with each other and builds trust.

Gary and Evelyn raised two sons together, had separate careers, and, in the last few years, launched a business together. They have learned a lot about how to make decisions jointly.

"We were pretty equal partners from the beginning," Evelyn explained. "I know in the business model sometimes you'll find the guy runs the business and the woman comes in and does the books and helps out. That was not our model. We were equal at home and in the business from the start. We each have our own set of projects and clients that we work on. Then we decide major things together."

To make it work, Gary goes on, "We also have a willingness to let things drop, if we can't agree. If there's something, either in our personal or business life, where we don't agree, we just don't make the decision—we don't make the decision until we agree. We're just lucky we have so many common shared interests and likes and dislikes that we usually do agree."

Manage Your Money Together

Couples in great marriages agree that no matter how much or how little money you have, you must share the important decisions on earning, spending, and saving. The income and your common assets belong to both of you jointly. You must learn how to make decisions together and balance each other's financial strengths and weaknesses.

NO SECRETS ABOUT MONEY

The first rule of money management is: No surprises and no secrets. Both of you need to have a full grasp of your financial picture. There should not be any secrets between the two of you, financial or otherwise. Keep each other informed. Even if one partner assumes primary responsibility for investing or paying bills, each needs to keep the other informed and involved. If you change jobs or start your own business, it will affect both of you—so both of you should take part in the decisions. You may find that your partner has enough distance on the project to be able to provide some valuable insights or caveats.

The first rule of money management is: No surprises and no secrets.

AGREE ON YOUR GOALS AND PRIORITIES

Discuss and come to an agreement on your short-term and long-term financial goals, expectations, and strategies. These will vary a great deal depending upon your age and stage of life. If you're still in college, your main financial goal may be to pay for your tuition next year. If you're at the beginning of a career, you might want to have a strategy for paying back student loans and saving for your first major purchases. If you are well established, you can take a more detailed look at your financial future.

No matter how meager or robust your assets, money decisions and plans need to be revisited regularly. Job and salary changes, shifts in the economy, plans about having children or the size of your family, unexpected expenses, and your own life stage and goals all affect your financial decisions. Many couples find the New Year or tax season to be good times to take stock of this aspect of your lives and, perhaps, consult professionals. You may want to review the questions on your financial attitudes (see pages 63–65 for a discussion of money issues in Chapter Four, "Agree on the Big Six") to see what you need to focus on and whether you both need to discuss matters with a friend, relative, or experienced professional.

Angela and Tim did not really feel great about how they handled money together until several years into their marriage. "We used to argue about money a lot," Tim recalls. "But then we came up with a new plan: a yearly budget in which we laid out everything—all our plans for spending and saving. Once a year, in November, we go over our budget for the coming year. In the beginning we'd do it month by month, and then each month we'd have arguments: 'We don't have money for this, we don't have money for that.'

"But now we both know the whole financial picture—what we have in stocks, savings, in the checkbook, in debts, and future expenses. So we don't really argue about money anymore."

Angela continues: "Having this plan made me feel more secure.

Money was a problem, because there were times when Tim was out of work, and I just didn't know what our money situation was. Not that either one of us spent a lot of money, because we didn't. Neither of us has a problem with gambling or anything like that. There just never seemed to be enough for our family of seven, you know?

"But now that I can see what there is, in black and white, I only spend what we have agreed to spend," Angela says. "So we don't have to argue anymore. The problem isn't how much money you have— we still don't have a lot. The issue is communication."

MAKE SURE YOUR PARTNER FEELS COMFORTABLE

If you are considering making a purchase that you will see or use nearly every day, like a piece of furniture or art, or the dishes or silverware, include your partner in the decision. That doesn't mean that every single financial move needs to be reviewed by both of you. But if you ask yourself, "Would my partner want to be involved in this decision?" and the answer is yes, take the time to talk it over beforehand.

Whenever you make a financial decision, stay within each other's comfort zone about spending and saving. Even if you have agreed that a purchase is your decision, think about how your partner will feel about the expenditure and err in the direction of safety.

SHOW RESPECT FOR YOUR DIFFERENCES

You are bound to find some differences in your attitudes about money. One person is often better at spending, the other at saving. One may be more fiscally conservative, the other more willing to take financial risks. That's to be expected. But the money belongs to you both. Whatever your differences, your relationship will stay strong if you come to an agreement about how you will work together to handle current finances and prepare for your financial future.

Think of your differences as opportunities to balance each other out and create greater financial stability for you both, rather than as sources of friction. Encourage each other to exercise whatever may be each of your financial strengths. If one of you is better organized, let that person handle the paperwork. If one of you is more cautious about spending, and you both have agreed that saving for your kids' college or a family vacation or retirement are important priorities, then the more cautious partner may want to take primary responsibility for overseeing the savings.

SEPARATE OR JOINT BANK ACCOUNTS AND CREDIT CARDS?

You may want to have three bank accounts: one main account for all major expenses, and two smaller accounts, one for each partner to use for personal weekly expenses, clothes, and other personal items, including presents for each other.

The main account can cover all basic expenses, such as rent/mortgage, food, child care, education, big household purchases, car payments, insurance, investments, vacations, etc. No matter who is in charge, you will need to talk over all nonroutine expenditures made from this account.

Keeping the smaller accounts separate allows each of you to have some privacy and autonomy—especially when it comes to buying your partner a present. Having your own account for that purpose may remind you to indulge your partner not just for holidays and birthdays, but also when you want to cheer him or her up and say, "I love you."

All the money in the accounts, no matter how big or small, should be shared jointly. But for many couples it works well when the responsibility for balancing each personal checkbook belongs to each partner separately.

Each of you should have your own credit card, too. It makes it unnecessary to carry a lot of cash and gives you a monthly record of what you spent. This also gives each partner privacy for buying the other gifts. And for both partners, but women especially, it is important to establish an independent credit record in one's own name, should anything happen to your partner. With credit cards, as with all expenditures, it is critical to stay within your jointly-agreed-upon budget and avoid debts if at all possible.

CREATE A BUDGET AND STICK TO IT

Don't strain your financial resources. With personal expenses, such as clothing, entertainment, and lunches, set a monthly and yearly limit for each of you and for the family—and stick to it. Avoid *all* unnecessary expenses, whether for household or personal items. If you find shopping irresistible, stay away from the malls. Find something else to do with your time—exercise, do some volunteer work, visit your mother. If you both respect your budget, you won't have endless discussions and conflicts over spending.

Agree not to overdraw bank accounts and do not go into credit card debt. Not only does such debt create unnecessary tension and anxiety for everyone, it is the most expensive way to borrow money. The high interest rate alone, which is easily double and triple normal loan rates, can wreck your budget.

SET SOME MONEY ASIDE FOR THE FUTURE

It is important to set a portion of your income aside on a regular basis for emergencies and future needs. You will not be able to achieve your goals unless you start saving early. Take advantage of the savings plans at your workplace—you're never too young to start a 401K or IRA. Save for happy occasions: trips, vacations, your own or your children's educational needs, a new car or household item, or even a new house. Prepare for unanticipated problems: medical emergencies, a relative who may need to borrow money, a need for extra cash in case you lose a job or decide to change careers.

Support Each Other's Career Goals

A great marriage can give both partners the financial and emotional security they need to do what they have always dreamed about. Having two potential incomes may enable one partner or both to go back to school to get an advanced degree. A loving and steadfast marriage partner can provide just the encouragement the other partner needs to try something new in their career. This may be why many people change jobs within a year of marriage—they feel secure enough to aim high and not settle.

Talk about the work you are doing (or thinking of doing) and the satisfaction you take in your career, as well as what might be missing and how you could make it better. Explore what kind of training, further education, or experiences you may need in order to reach your goals.

Perhaps you need to move to another city or region, or apply your experience to a new, growing field. Maybe you need to switch to part-time work, or stop working, as you write a book or have children. You need to rethink your work arrangements when you begin a family (see the next chapter of for ideas on work/family balance). Discuss how you can actively support each other—perhaps lending a hand with a new business or using your skills to help the other in a challenging new position—so that you both can reach your goals.

RESPECT EACH OTHER'S HOPES AND DREAMS

What is important in balancing your career with your partner's is that you each feel your hopes and dreams are respected and that you balance your needs fairly over time.

You may not always be able to pursue your dreams at the same time. One of you may need to slow your career while the other takes on a new challenge that includes lots of travel or a foreign assignment. One of you may have to live in a place you may not want to settle down in forever, to help the other. You may need to take on extra assignments if you've decided one of you will stay home full time to care for a new baby.

If you both feel confident that the other's turn will come, then you will be able to make the best of each stage as you pass through it. Trusting each other to take turns fairly is vital to a happy marriage. These periods of growth and change, as your work patterns and goals change, can be among the most exciting and productive times in your lives.

What is important in balancing your career with your partner's is that you each feel your hopes and dreams are respected and that you balance your needs fairly over time.

When Carrie and Frank got married, they thought they'd both go back to school to get Ph.D.'s. But when they added up their bills, it was clear that one of them would have to keep working. As Carrie recalls it, "I realized that the Ph.D. meant more to Frank's career path and his ego at the time than it did to mine. So I worked while he studied. But

Frank supported me in a lot of other ways throughout my work."

Carrie went on to have a highly successful career, working as an executive director at a major medical school. She was even more successful than Frank was financially. "Things often even out in the end," Carrie says.

Share the Household Chores

When it comes to managing the household, everybody should contribute something. Nobody gets away with doing nothing inside the home, no matter what each of you earns or contributes outside the house. Even if only one of you has a job, the job should not be an excuse to avoid pitching in. When both of you roll up your sleeves to do chores, the household becomes something that belongs to both of you and that you both have a stake in. It's how you make a house a home, and it's also how you teach your children to become good partners when they grow up. You have to be prepared to do your fair share of things you love to do—and some things you don't much like doing, as well

---

Nobody gets away with doing nothing inside the home, no matter what each of you earns or contributes outside the house. That's how the household becomes something that belongs to both of you. It's how you make a house a home

---

DIVIDE THE LABOR IN A WAY THAT MAKES BOTH OF YOU HAPPY

Find out what you each love to do and encourage each other to do it. If he loves to cook, then you can do the cleaning up. If she likes to do yard work, then you can do the shopping. Try not to keep score. If you have the feeling your partner is doing more than you are, you are probably right. Pitch in and do a little more yourself. Make sure you each get to do some things you love and share the rest of what has to be done. Review your division of labor periodically. Be willing to make changes to keep up with your changing interests, needs, and preferences.

Joanne says that she and Dean do not share everything equally, but they have worked out a plan that makes them both very happy.

"I do most of the taking care of the kids and dinners, and he does the coffee in the morning. I don't interfere at all with this, because this is his way of making love to me. He makes it just the way I like it, with the Irish Cream in it—you know, the flavored creamers. And he brings it up and puts it on my desk. That's a very important thing to do!

"He also keeps the animals happy. He lets the dog out, feeds the dog, the cat, and the bird. He takes care of the automobiles and the plumbing and the electricity. He keeps my computer running really well.

"Sometimes we clean the house together—but just for an hour. We'll say, okay, it's one hour of cleaning, everybody get as much done in that hour, and then we're done. The house can wait."

CHORES ARE A CHANCE TO SHOW YOUR LOVE

Happy couples say they do not think of household chores as one more piece of drudgery to be endured. They look at each chore as one more opportunity to make their spouse's life easier. Taking care of the house shows how much you respect and love your partner.

No matter how much you earn or how hard your day was, you shouldn't be sitting there reading the newspaper if your partner is working hard in the next room. You should be asking yourself and your partner, "What can I do to help?" Once you look at chores this way, even taking out the garbage can take on new appeal. You may even find yourselves tempted to do more than your share, just to please your spouse. And not leaving your spouse stuck with it makes you feel good.

Nick and Claudia try to split the chores, though they acknowledge things can't always be perfectly equal. "We work very, very hard to share fifty-fifty on most things from housekeeping, to children and finances," Claudia says. Nick adds: "I have to admit, if we get to sixty-forty—Claudia doing sixty and me doing forty—then we're doing okay. But if we slip below sixty-forty, we squabble. So we really try to do fifty-fifty."

SHOW YOUR PARTNER GRATITUDE

Happy couples say they do one more thing when it comes to household chores—they remember to show their partner gratitude for doing his or her daily share. Even when they have come to an agreement on who does what, they don't take each other's contribution for granted. They express their thanks, especially if their partner has taken over part of their chores on occasion. *It is vitally important to let your spouse know how much you appreciate it when he or she makes your life a little easier and better.*

Joyce says that she and Harry realized early on not to take each other for granted.

"We quickly figured out that we should tell each other how much we liked the job they did—even if it was just doing what we were supposed to be doing to keep things rolling along. That way, we each tried a little harder to please each other. And when it came to the jobs nobody liked, like cleaning the bathroom, we took turns."

CHAPTER NINE

Enjoy Raising Children: Extend Your Love

One of the best things any couple can do for their children is to love each other and show their children, by example, what it is to have a great marriage.

—GERARD LEEDS

HAVING CHILDREN CAN BRING YOU CLOSER together than anything you have experienced since you first fell in love. It is hard to describe the depth and intensity of love having a child can evoke in a parent until you hold your own child in your arms. It is a love you hardly knew you were capable of feeling. Your love for your spouse also expands—just when you thought it couldn't get any bigger or better. For couples in great marriages, raising children together deepens their relationship in ways they hardly could have anticipated—and in ways they would never change.

Children also bring to a marriage a greater sense of responsibility than ever before. "I never knew how much fun or how much hard work kids could be until we had them," says Dan, father of four. You face a whole new set of ever-changing challenges to deal with, as you balance the work and decision making of child rearing while maintaining a strong bond as a couple. Job decisions, lifestyle, and religious views can take on a whole new dimension once you have to think not simply about how you want to live but what you care to pass along to your children, as well. Having fun together becomes more important than ever as it is the glue that keeps a family close.

Are You Ready to Have Children?

Only a few generations ago, people married younger than they do today and tended to have children right away. They didn't wait until they had established themselves in their careers or saved a great deal of money. Today, many couples are marrying several years later and having children later, too.

The time is right when you both really want to have children, feel that you are mature and capable enough to raise them, and are prepared to change your lives.

No one can say which path is better. There is no one formula for "the best time to have children." There is no magic number of months or years after you are married that you should wait before you can be confident that you are ready to begin a family.

The time is right when you both really want to have children, feel that you are capable and mature enough to raise them, are happy about your relationship (and are not thinking that children will "fix" anything that is wrong between you), and are prepared to change your lives. The timing also depends upon whether it is more important to you to be a bit older and established in your career first, or to be young, energetic, and adaptable when your children are young. Whether you start a family sooner or later can also depend upon how many children you expect to have, health and fertility issues, support you have from friends and family, and any other issues that are particularly important to one or both of you. On the financial side, having the stability that comes with steady income, health insurance, and at least some savings can ease the challenges that comes with this new stage of life.

So Many Ways to Balance Work and Family

Raising a baby should be a shared activity. Even if one partner assumes the role of primary caregiver and the other works outside the home, the happiest couples say they both have taken an active, hands-on role in the care and nurturing of their children from infancy on.

"It didn't matter how many hours my husband worked, he loved to come home and give the baby her bath and then cuddle her and give her a bottle," recalls Leslie, married to George for fourteen years.

Couples find that many different career-family arrangements work for them. Which work patterns seem right for you? Will you both work outside the home, or will one of you work part-time or not at all? Will you share child rearing equally or will one of you assume primary responsibility? What kind of child care, if any, do you think is best? What kind of care is available near you and what can you afford: a child care center, family day care, a nanny, an *au pair*, a parents' babysitting co-op? Can grandparents or other relatives offer any help? There are many options:

- Both of you may work outside the home, which means you will have to determine which child care options are right for your family.
- One of you may want to seek out work at a company that offers high-quality, on-site child care.
- One of the spouses may work outside the home while the other may decide to stay home full-time to take care of the children.
- One or both of you may work from home some or part of the time to have more flexibility and time with your children.
- Each parent might choose to work part-time and to stay at home the rest of the time to care for the children, with or without child-care support.

No choice is set in stone. When the kids are young, one parent may want to stay at home to take primary day-to-day responsibility for their care. Often this is the mother, but today many fathers pick this option, too. Sometimes a parent combines this role with part-time work or a business that can be run from home. When the kids are older, that spouse may go back to his or her career or find a new career to pursue with even more intensity than before. No matter which choice you make, you also have to have a backup plan for emergencies. When your child gets sick at the last minute, or the caregiver does—and it will happen—it shouldn't always fall to one parent or the other to do the fill-in caregiving.

You have to take the long view when it comes to work-family balance so that both partners feel the choices they make are fair and equal in the long run. Most important, if you treat each other's goals and aspirations with respect and support, you will both be satisfied in the end and feel as if you have achieved a balance that strengthens you both—and your marriage.

How Happy Couples Share Work and Family

In the following examples, you will notice that both partners believe they are making an important contribution to the welfare of the family. Both agree that they should share the job of raising the children—even if one assumes a bigger role than the other at times. And they both regard the work they do as vital to their family's welfare.

HUSBAND WORKS, WIFE STAYS AT HOME

Judy and Jim have been married for seventeen years. Judy says she worked for a long time before her daughter came along and she was ready for a break.

"I didn't want to miss those precious first few years. I was lucky because Jim earned enough to support us and I could stay at home with Zoe. I figured I could make up that career time, but I couldn't make up my daughter's first few milestones, like when she said her first words and took her first steps.

"Then we had Donald, two years later. I went back to work when Zoe was six, and Donald was four—she was in kindergarten and he was in child care. But I kept worrying about the kids when I was at work, and I felt guilty when I was at home that I should be doing some planning for work projects. Also, I kept having child-care troubles. Donald didn't seem happy in the center, and I kept losing babysitters and couldn't find someone dependable to take care of them when they got home from school. Besides, I was paying almost as much as I earned in child care expenses. So I quit again and stayed home until they both got to high school.

"I'm back at work now. Sometimes it is still a juggling act—Jim and I have to make sure they call us up as soon as they get home. But I am glad to be back in the office where I can talk with adults, for a change, and make new friends. And Zoe will be off to college next year, so the extra income will be a big help."

WIFE WORKS, HUSBAND STAYS HOME

John had a job at a newspaper before he and Ivy had children. But her career as a college professor proved to be more lucrative and satisfying than his. So when the kids came along, John was happy to stay at home.

"After a few years I started a small landscaping business out of the house, designing and planting the grounds of a few residences in our neighborhood. On the days when Ivy didn't have to be on campus all day, I could take on a few clients. That gave me a little income, but meant we wouldn't have to hire anyone to look after the kids—except when we went out on a date together at night. And we were both always there for the family dinners—we thought that was important for the kids and for our family.

"We liked that we both got to spend time with our kids as they grew up. Some guys I meet think the choices I made were a little odd. Not too many men stay at home with the kids—it's still new territory. But Ivy and I are happy about it—and that's all that counts."

HUSBAND AND WIFE BOTH SHARE WORK AND CHILD CARE

David and Carla decided they would share everything as evenly as they could—work, family, and time for fun. "In the morning, I take the two older children to elementary school," David says. "I try to leave an extra twenty minutes so the three of us can play outside before I have to say good-bye. Carla takes the baby to the day-care center and does the same thing—she sits down with Amy and gets her settled in before taking off for work. Carla also takes Fridays off to spend the day with Amy and the other kids when they get home."

Carla adds: "We have a babysitter who picks all three kids up after school and takes care of them until we get home. Then we try to have dinner together most nights. David loves to cook; he says it relaxes him. I do the dishes while he gets the kids washed up and ready for bed. We trade off reading to them at night because we both love that part. Some nights we are so tired we almost fall asleep in the middle of a page. But most days we count ourselves pretty lucky that we can both keep up with our careers and not miss out on the joy of watching our kids grow up."

David continues: "When the babysitter gets sick it throws our lives into turmoil. But we have learned that we have to have a list of backup babysitters and relatives who can come at the last minute. If there's nobody to help us, we try to take turns changing our work schedules so it isn't always Carla or me who has to fill the child-care gap."

There are endless variations for combining work schedules with time at home. As the children get older and spend more time in school, sometimes a third caregiver beyond the parents enters the work-family balancing act.

Jeff and Lindsay, who have three children, both work part-time so they can share the child rearing, too.

"I take Mondays off, Lindsay takes Fridays off, to stay home and be with the kids," Jeff says. "For the middle three days the little one is in day care and the older kids are in school. It's an unusual arrangement, but it works for us. Both Lindsay and I really look forward to those days off from work—we get to take time to really appreciate the kids, and we think they benefit, too."

Agree on How to Handle Religious Differences in the Family

Religion and spirituality can provide an enormously satisfying source of strength, comfort, and stability for the whole family. It can be a deeply uniting force, whether you share the same religion or not. But as we discussed in Chapter Four, "Agree on the Big Six" (p. 59), this is an aspect of your relationship that can cause a lot of tension if it is not carefully planned. Even when you're comfortable with the role religion plays in your life as a couple, the arrival of children can bring up new issues and choices. Which rituals and practices do you want to follow? Do you want a naming ceremony? Baptism? Circumcision? Do you go to services daily? Weekly? On holidays? No matter what you decide, if you agree on how you will approach religion with your children, you can provide a stable environment and an enduring way to live together happily.

Here are the stories of five couples. They had differing religious beliefs before marriage but were all able to make religion work to bring their families closer.

SARAH AND PATRICK: DIFFERENT RELIGIONS

Sarah and Patrick recognized from the moment they set eyes on each other in college that they came from very different religious backgrounds. That was part of the attraction. She had the dark curly hair, olive skin, and hazel eyes of her ancestors, Jews from Eastern Europe. He had "the map of Ireland on his face," as is often said of light-skinned, blue-eyed males with round moon faces who are of Irish Catholic descent.

They agreed, early on, that if they had children, they would expose them to both religions and let the children see what faith they would choose as adults themselves.

They did ultimately have two boys. The older one chose to go through the Jewish ceremony of a Bar Mitzvah. The younger one occasionally attends church services, but hasn't made up his mind yet. The whole family lights the Chanukah candles together and a week or two later attends midnight Mass for Christmas as a family. They exchange presents and have big special dinners for both holidays. Sarah and Patrick are pleased to share the richness of two traditions with each other, their children, and both families.

MOHAMMED AND DIANA: DIFFERENT RELIGIONS, ONE PARTNER CONVERTS

Mohammed loved everything about Diana, including her sweet Southern accent. But he also knew that it was important to him to raise their children in the Muslim faith. So Diana converted. They have three children, all of whom go to mosque with him. And Mohammed has to admit that on some issues of Muslim practice and belief, as laid out in the Koran, Diana may just know more than he does. He couldn't be happier. His parents are, too.

133

GENE AND ELLEN: SAME RELIGION, DIFFERENT PRACTICES

Gene and Ellen were both raised in Cleveland; both were Protestant. But they felt very differently about how they wanted to follow their faith. To put it simply, Ellen felt a lot more religious than Gene did. She wanted to attend services every week. He would have been just as happy seeing the inside of a church only a few times a year.

But when they had children, they agreed upon a middle ground. The whole family attends church together at least once or twice a month.

Gene and Ellen both feel that they have benefited by each adapting to the other. Neither feels as if they have had to sacrifice their identity.

"I probably wouldn't have bothered going if Ellen didn't want to," Gene says. "But I believe it has added a lot to the closeness our family feels."

JAMES AND SALLY: NEITHER PARTNER PRACTICES RELIGION

James and Sally have different religions, but one thing in common: they both grew up in households where religion was not very important. That's just how they both liked it. They were happy to sleep in on Sundays. And when their four children came along, the shared Sunday ritual was a whopping big breakfast together. They have tried to instill in their children an understanding of and tolerance for all religions. They have told each of them it is up to them to explore whatever religion they might find of interest.

JEFF AND LINDA: ONE RELIGION CHOSEN FOR THE FAMILY

Jeff and Linda did not feel it was necessary for either of them to convert to the other's religion. But they did think it would be better to bring the children up with one faith. Though Jeff is Lutheran, he agreed that the children should follow the religion that Anne grew up with.

So they all go to the Episcopalian Church not far from their home in Annapolis. The two girls have just been confirmed and the youngest boy has a part in the Christmas pageant. "I don't feel as if I made any sacrifice at all," says Jeff. "It makes us feel more solidly like a family to all go together on Sundays. I think we made the right choice for us."

Teach Your Children the Same Values That Attracted You to Each Other

Both parents serve as role models. Your words as well as your deeds provide the guidelines for your children to follow as they grow into adults who share your highest values. The ways you teach and discipline them are also an expression of your values that will affect their entire lives.

Remember to put love and respect in all your interactions with your children, and the rest will follow.

Remember to put love and respect in all your interactions with your children, and the rest will follow.

Have Meals Together Every Day

The dinner table is where you build a cohesive family. It is where you teach without self-consciously teaching. As you eat, you share experiences, opinions, values, and plans for the future, so that children feel an integral part of the family. Your children learn to express themselves with adults and other children. They learn table manners and, even more important, social graces, such as how polite conversation is conducted. If you model this behavior for them, they also learn how to listen to the ideas of others and respectfully voice their own thoughts and opinions. You teach your children values by what you say, what you do, and what you expect from them.

Read to Your Children from the Day They Are Born

Infants may not understand the words, but they take comfort in the sound of your voice. They also learn the basics of reading skills by hearing the rhythms of language. And as they grow up, they learn to think of reading as something associated with warm and loving family togetherness. What better way to instill a lifelong love of reading?

Be Affectionate with Your Whole Family

Research shows that infants learn and grow best when held and touched. One famous study on children in an orphanage revealed that when infants are not held and touched, they are not simply emotionally hurt, they are physically stunted—they do not grow normally. All of us—children and parents alike—flourish with affection. You've seen the bumper stickers, "Did you hug your kids today?" Now go and do it. The best example you can set for your kids is to hug them and your partner as well.

Husbands and wives should feel comfortable about showing affection for each other in front of the children. Though kids love to groan and mock their parents when they dance together or kiss in the kitchen, such displays can reassure them that their parents' marriage is strong. It reinforces the message that a normal and healthy part of love, at all ages, includes affection.

Hugs, cuddles, and pats on the back should not be reserved for special occasions or accomplishments. Dispense your affection liberally. It solidifies your bond with your children and fosters a loving closeness that will help you both through the difficult stages of growing up, and improve your relationship throughout your lives.

Involve the Children from the Earliest Age in Household Chores

Very young children are delighted to help you load the dryer and sort socks or set the table. Older children can do the dishes, take out the garbage, rake leaves and mow the lawn, make their beds, and feed and walk the dog.

Everybody has to learn that they can be a useful member of the family, take responsibility, and contribute a share. It makes each member of the family feel important and valued. It shows the children that everybody has to contribute to the success of the family. It also helps them become good partners, husbands, and wives later on.

Encourage the Children to Help Each Other, Too

The older children can help the younger ones learn to do more difficult chores around the house. They can also help the younger ones with their homework. The younger ones can reciprocate by sometimes taking over the chores of the big brother or sister. They all learn how to cooperate and work together to get the work done.

Take Your Children to Work or on a Business Trip with You

There is no better way for children to learn more about what their parents do all day than to see you on the job. They can understand why sometimes Mom or Dad might have to come home late when work demands it. They also get a better idea of what the world of work might hold for them one day.

Go to Their School Activities, Sports Events, and Extracurricular Activities

Sometimes just showing up is enough. It shows your children that you care enough about them to take the time to see what they're doing. And it helps the schools, which depend upon parent volunteers and support for many student activities during and after school. Your participation lets your kids know how important school is in their lives. It also gives you insight into your kids' characters, their friends, and the texture of their lives.

Linda and Nick feel that they each bring different—but equally important—qualities to their three children's lives. "Linda has this very, very deep, strong, nurturing quality in her," Nick says. "Especially as a mother. She's really good at being with our kids, nurturing them, reading with them, really spending quality time with our children. I've learned to be that way, but I wasn't that way before. Being with Linda strengthens that part of me. I like that."

Linda adds, "It's true, but Nick does that for me, too. I remember asking myself last time we went on vacation, *If Nick weren't here, would I make all this effort to go skiing with our kids?* Maybe I would, but I know it wouldn't be anywhere near as much fun as it is with

Nick. He helps me have a lot more fun with the kids because he's just so fun to be with."

Discipline Your Children Wisely, in Age-Appropriate Ways

As humans, we don't come programmed with the knowledge we need to survive. Adults need to teach children how to live a good life and be reasonable, participating citizens. From sleeping through the night to toilet training, sharing, and getting along with siblings and friends, as parents we need to teach our children in age-appropriate ways.

You and your spouse need to agree on what is acceptable behavior and establish clear rules for your children to follow. If you set consistent limits and model good behavior, they will know what is expected of them. There is no right or wrong approach, as long as you settle on one that works with your children, helps them become responsible human beings you can be proud of, and makes you both comfortable. When you face decisions together, you are more likely to make sound choices that encourage your children's healthy development without spoiling them.

Aim to be firm, reasonable, and fair. You also want to be consistent from child to child. However, each child has unique needs and strengths and so there are times when being "fair" doesn't mean being "the same." Most important, you both should be united as parents. Don't contradict each other on discipline matters in front of the child.

Raising children, like other parts of your life, involves learning and evolving as you go.

It isn't necessary to have all the answers before you have children, or even after you have your baby cradled in your arms. Raising children, like other parts of your life, involves learning and evolving as you go. If you have questions of what to do or concerns about your children, read books, talk with other parents, and consult with your pediatrician and your children's teachers to see if counseling, physical therapy, educational testing, or tutors may be necessary.

Have Fun with Your Children and Each Other

Children can feel like an enormous responsibility. You want so much to raise them right. But don't let yourself get overwhelmed by the seriousness of the task. Remember to share with them the things you both value the most, bring them in on some of your inside jokes and rituals, and forge new rituals that belong to the whole family.

Part of the fun of having children is that sometimes you wonder who is teaching whom the important life lessons. Your children are always watching you, listening and learning, even when they don't seem to be. You don't discover that until those surprising moments when they turn the tables and teach you what's really important about living and loving.

"Gerry and I had one of those great 'turn-the-tables' moments on a family vacation, when our five kids were still small," Lilo recalls. "After a very long, cramped car trip, the kids poured out of the car and let loose all their pent-up energy by fighting and wrestling each other. My cousin, Lilliane, who joined us at the hotel in Canada, was appalled by the ruckus.

"'Well, what would you advise to stop them from fighting?' I asked my cousin, who also happened to be a brilliant psychologist. Lilliane said she didn't know how to stop older kids, but if the children were younger and throwing a temper tantrum, then the mother should just go to the bathroom, turn on the TV, or sit down and read a book.

"That night, Gerry and I had a fight. The kids were right there in the room with us because we were all staying in a hotel suite. After a couple of minutes we noticed that one child got up and turned on the TV, one went off to the bathroom, and a third sat down and started reading a book.

"It worked. We all laughed so much we stopped fighting. And even today, when any of us mentions that night, we all still have a good laugh remembering it."

From the very start, while you have the chance to influence your children's attitudes and preferences, teach them to enjoy the things you love—hiking, concerts, playing ball, traveling, whatever—so you can all keep doing these things as a family. Playing sports together, discussing books or politics, taking walks, going on vacations, laughing together about shared memories, are all ways to enjoy each other, learn more about each other, and get closer as a family. If you do that early on, you will all continue to have great fun together all your lives.

Make Time for the Two of You, As a Couple

No matter how much fun you are having with your children, or how much energy and time they take up, don't forget to leave time for your partner—just you two. Keep doing the things you always enjoyed doing together. Enjoy your social life, your hobbies, and your couple time. You shouldn't have to feel as if you are sacrificing your life to raise your children.

Save time for each other—to talk, to have sex, to go out on a picnic or just take a walk. Set aside an uninterrupted period of time to make plans for the future, your next job, your next vacation. You need to sit down together and talk as adults, who have lives outside those of your children, as you had when you first met.

The best gift you can give your children, now and for their lifetime, is to show them how happy married partners can make each other.

The best gift you can give your children, now and for their lifetime, is to show them how happy married partners can make each other. Keeping your relationship with your partner strong, loving, and affectionate provides your children with the love and stability they need to grow up happy and healthy. Equally important, it provides them with the best possible model of a marriage—the kind, if they're lucky, they will have when they grow up, too.

Francine and Donald have learned a great deal about their marriage as they have raised three children. "For many years when the kids were babies, I always thought my job was to put the kids first," Francine says. "And I think Donald felt his job was to put the job first because he wanted to do well for his family. And we didn't take a vacation for six years because money was tight.

"We lost sight of each other in all that, and it got to a point where communication between us was so poor I was reading every self-help book for marriage imaginable, trying to fix it," Francine recalls.

"What we learned is that no matter what your financial circumstances, you have to make time for each other, to remember why you hooked up in the first place," Francine says. "So now we have regular date nights. We go to this little restaurant where they have sofas in the bar area and we just sit and we talk, for hours, and really enjoy each other's company. We connect with each other and share something together that's just for us. That's what keeps our whole family together."

Donald adds: "I believe that whatever we leave our children financially is not our legacy. Our real lasting legacy is the type of people that they become and carry forward with their children. So for future generations, I think the most influence you can have is the way you raise your children and the example you set for them by having a great marriage."

CHAPTER TEN

Build a Happy, Healthy Life Together: Take Care of Yourselves, Your Friends, and Your Community

> Life has taught us that love does not consist in gazing at each other but in looking outward together in the same direction.
>
> — ANTOINE DE SAINT-EXUPERY, *The Litte Prince*

A HAPPY LIFE DEPENDS NOT ONLY ON DOING everything with love and respect between the two of you, but also on helping each other extend your circle of love and good will beyond the two of you. There are four areas where you will find the lucky coincidence that doing what's *good* for each of you also does *good* for both of you, and the world around you.

- **Focus on the fun**—find recreational activities that you both love and enjoy doing them together.
- **Get healthy and stay that way**—it's something you do for your own well-being and for your partner's benefit, too.
- **Make his or her friends your friends, too**—and connect with both of your extended families—it enriches and strengthens you and your relationship.
- **Give something back to the community around you**—getting involved *outside* your relationship brings the greatest rewards and love back *into* your relationship.

Focus on the Fun

A person living to age seventy has 613,000 hours of life. This is too long a period not to have fun.

—ANONYMOUS

One of the pillars of a great relationship is sharing common passions and pursuits. Happy couples usually enjoy several interests that bring them together in their free time. Outdoor adventures like hiking, biking, skiing, golf, camping, taking walks, gardening, or indoor activities like reading books, playing poker, watching TV, making love, visiting friends, or discussing movies all bring couples closer. They broaden your understanding and appreciation of each other—beyond the usual world of work and home.

Another side benefit—shared activities are just plain fun. The sign of truly happily married couples is that they are looking for fun even when they are doing ordinary, everyday chores.

"We read books together, we spend so many hours talking to each other on the phone that we feel like teenagers again," says Kathryn, who is in her seventh year of marriage to Sam, after both had unhappy first marriages. Sam sums it up: "In the beginning, we had so much fun just being together we almost felt guilty."

As you play and enjoy exercise, sports, or leisure activities together, you have the opportunity to learn new skills and spur each other on to greater heights. When you learn about your partner's passions and join in on occasion, you may just find that his or her love of cooking, exercising, antiquing, gardening, or salsa dancing rubs off on you. You can tap into abilities you might never have realized you had.

Learn and Grow—Together

When you take a class together, you benefit from the intellectual stimulation at the same time you cut through daily routines and familiarity. It gives you a chance to broaden your knowledge and enjoy each other's insights and abilities in a fresh context. If you happen to have met during college, it reconnects you to that wonderful time.

Having a shared project enables you to work toward something challenging and significant in your lives.

Some couples take on more ambitious goals together, such as starting a community garden, renovating a house, or getting involved with a not-for-profit organization. Having a shared project enables you to work toward something challenging and significant in your lives. You learn about each other's strengths. You also get to show off your new expertise in front of each other and receive validation together. By working jointly toward a long-term goal you are building something solid together.

"Lilo and I went back for a master's degree together," Gerry explains. "It was some of the most fun we've had. It took us five years but we enjoyed every minute of it. We had one night a week when Lilo's mother stayed at the house and we went out without feeling guilty—we always went out to dinner before or after the class, too, to make it a real night out.

"We took classes in whatever seemed intriguing—from English literature to foreign policy. We even persuaded one of our teachers to let us write our term paper together. Lilo liked the facts, I liked fiction, so she did the research and I wrote the paper. We played to each other's strengths—and it brought us closer together."

One thing is certain: When you have fun together, whether you simply take a walk after dinner or travel to exotic parts of the world, you have a chance to relax, learn, and grow together. That's critical for deepening intimacy further. Doing something you both enjoy sets a great example for your children and creates an emotional bond that deepens your love and commitment to each other.

Date Nights

You have probably heard other couples say that they try to go out on dates as often as they can to keep their marriage romantic. The reason you have heard about it is that it works.

It is so easy to get caught up in the busy-ness and seriousness of day-to-day living that you may forget to take a break—together. If you schedule a regular, weekly night out for just the two of you—even if only for a few hours—you'll be glad you did.

David and Carla, married fourteen years, have three young children, which makes it especially important for them to get away by themselves. Once a week, after dinner, they go to a funny little inn thirty minutes from their house, where the only thing people do is sprawl on couches, smoke cigars, and sip brandy.

"Neither David nor I smoke cigars, but for just a couple of hours, after dinner, we sip our brandy, agree not to discuss the children at all, and just engage in completely grown-up conversation," says Carla. "We talk about the news, our next vacation, our dreams, what we would do if we had three wishes. We flirt with each other and mostly we make each other laugh. Sometimes, when we get back home, we feel better than if we'd gone on a week's vacation. And it's a whole lot cheaper."

Spend Time Alone, Too

Happy couples aren't stuck together like Velcro. They don't have to do everything together. It is important to respect each other's privacy and to give each other time alone. Much as you have in common, each of you needs to be able to use your creativity and find fulfillment individually. Whether you pursue your own interests in sports, the arts, playing an instrument, reading a good book, baking a cake, or just going out to lunch with friends—most people need the time and freedom to do things on their own.

Happy couples aren't stuck together like Velcro. It is important to respect each other's privacy and to give each other time alone.

When you feel strong, accomplished, and happy as an individual, that happiness and confidence will carry over into your relationship. When you show your partner respect for his or her personal pursuits, it can only strengthen the bond between you.

"We do pretty much everything together—except shopping," says Joyce. "We go walking. We play tennis. We like talking together, taking walks.

"But we also like to do a few things alone. I have more fun going shopping with my girlfriends."

"She sometimes encourages me to go skiing with the guys on weekends because she doesn't like skiing," says Harry. "That works out fine for both of us."

Happy couples are able to respect each other's independence while still being strongly united as a couple.

"There are some Saturdays when neither of us knows what the other is doing all day," says Richard, married seventeen years. "We are busy taking classes and volunteering in a literacy program. And many weekday evenings we are each with our separate friends or with clients."

"Richard and I are married to each other—we don't own one another," adds Marilyn.

"But every Wednesday night is our 'date night,' so we are sure to get together in the middle of the week," Richard continues. "And then Friday, Saturday, and Sunday nights we are almost always together—often just the two of us relaxing at home or out for a simple dinner or a movie."

Giving each other breathing space is critical. The wonderful irony is that this healthy separation will bring you closer together. It's a matter of *differentiation*, as we discussed in Chapter Two, "Date with Purpose" (p. 25). The happiest couples are able to strike the right balance between their need for togetherness and their need for doing things on their own. The more developed and mature they become as individuals, the stronger and better a marriage partner they become. As Shakespeare summed it up in Hamlet: "This above all, to thine own self be true, And it must follow, as the night the day, Thou cannot then be false to any man."

Jane and Lee have been careful to encourage each other to develop independent interests and talents.

"I really credit our individual growth for the success of our marriage," Lee says, after thirty-eight years of marriage. "I absolutely do,

147

and I think that any couple that doesn't allow each person to develop is going to wake up one morning, whether it's two years, ten years, or twenty years later, and say, 'God, I was always doing everything for you, I never did anything for me.' We realized it's not fair to really blame the other person for that when you chose it yourself."

"At the beginning of our relationship," Jane adds, "each time I tried something new, like a new hobby, it caused a little turmoil. Lee had to get used to the idea of my having time away—and I did, too. But it always turned out to be just wonderful afterward. Now, even when we're on vacation, we try to give the other a chance to do something alone, on a daily basis. Lee has to make time to write. And I have to look for quilting fabrics. We understand that now, but we didn't at first. And it brings us closer."

Vacations Are Vital—With and Without the Children

If you think of vacations as luxuries, think again. Happy couples say that they are absolutely essential to a great marriage. Because vacations are so important to keeping fun and pleasure alive in your marriage, they should be built into your budget. They don't have to cost a fortune to work their magic. They just have to provide you both with a break from the routine.

There's nothing like a moonlit walk along a beach, bare feet sinking into the sand, arms around each other's waists—far from the house, the bills, the busy schedules—to remind you how good life together can be, and will be for many years to come. Even when you have children, it is important now and then to try to get away together, just as a couple. As Mignon McLaughlin, an American journalist and author, once quipped, "A successful marriage requires falling in love many times, and always with the same person."

"We try every few months to get away for a weekend—or at least for a night alone," says Beth. "We call up my mother, who luckily lives nearby, and she babysits for our four kids while we go off to a bed-and-breakfast and do whatever pleases the two of us. Some weekends we never get out bed, except to go out to eat."

Vacations with the kids can build family spirit and add new dimensions to your relationship with your spouse and with your children, too. Everybody tends to be more relaxed than usual on vacation. Just being away from school activities and work deadlines tends to bring out the best in everyone. You reinforce your admiration for your spouse as a creative, fun-loving parent and partner. You create joyous memories that deepen your bonds with your children, as well.

Vacations also provide opportunities to educate your children in unusual and entertaining ways. What better way to learn about the environment than on a camping trip to a national forest or a rafting trip on a river? When you see each other operating in a new setting and using skills that may not come into play at home, it allows family members to break out of the old patterns of interaction at home and gain new respect for each other's abilities.

Beth and David love to travel. "Recently we've started to do more traveling because all the kids are living on their own," David says. "We've been to Israel, Sweden, London, and Paris. When we were planning our last trip to Singapore, Thailand, and Japan, our younger daughter thought it sounded so exciting that she asked if she could come along, too. She did! That was just great."

Get Healthy and Stay That Way

In a happy marriage, staying healthy is something both partners do—for themselves *and* for each other. The healthier each spouse is in mind, body, and spirit, the healthier and stronger the marriage will be:

- You will feel more energetic and alive, so you will be more active and fun company for each other.
- You will look more attractive if you're healthy and fit, so you will continue to be attracted to each other.
- You will cope better with stress, so you will be pleasanter, more relaxed, and better able to share your good moods with each other.
- And best of all, you will live healthier longer, so you will have the most time possible to enjoy your partner and your life together.

Small changes in your daily life can yield big improvements. Simply eating healthy foods, getting enough sleep, handling stress before it builds up, and walking a half hour every day can make a huge difference in your own life—and in your life together. It can make all the difference in your marriage.

The healthier each spouse is in mind, body, and spirit, the healthier and stronger the marriage will be.

Seven Rules for Staying Healthy

When you take care of yourself, you bring your best self to your relationship. You have more energy and enthusiasm for everyone and everything around you. Everyone benefits. Here are seven simple rules for staying healthy in mind, body, and spirit.

1. Eat a healthy diet.
2. Get enough sleep.
3. Exercise regularly.
4. Make time for recreational activities.
5. Don't smoke or abuse alcohol or drugs.
6. Be positive—optimists live longer.
7. Reduce stress and relax.

For more detailed information on each of these seven rules for healthy living, turn to "A Wellness Primer" at the end of the book.

Extend Your Circle of Friends and Family

Love builds bridges where there are none.

—R. H. Delaney

Happy couples say both partners try very hard to make *their partner's* friends and family *their* friends and family. Don't expect it to happen overnight; it can take time and sometimes a good deal of patience. But the effort is worth it. Just as your relationship gets stronger with each day you get to know and love each other better, incorporating these new friends and family can make your relationship stronger, too.

Keep things in perspective. While it's very important to accommodate both of your parents and relatives as much as possible, in the end, your life as a couple comes first. Patterns of interaction that may have been fine when you were single may not be ideal now that you're a couple. You may no longer want to go to your parents' house for dinner every Sunday. You both may want to spend some Sundays by yourselves, just the two of you and perhaps your children. Be generous with your time, but also set limits to protect your relationship. Most of all, be patient. It can take a while for everyone to adjust to new family dynamics.

"Gerry and I are very thankful my mother was so understanding," Lilo says. "When we got married, I was the only remaining child my parents had and they didn't want me to feel guilty about spending less time with them. My mother said to me that day, 'From now on I'll be second fiddle—your husband will come first. That's the way it should be.' With an attitude like that on her part, we established a wonderful relationship in which she was always there for us and our children—and we were always there for her."

Holidays Present Challenges

Holidays have to be planned with great care. Which in-laws do you go to for Thanksgiving? For religious holidays? Over vacation? Start well in advance of the holidays to talk over with each other what your holiday plans will be. Here again, if you both take the long view, it will be easier to achieve balance and fairness over the course of years.

My Friends... Your Friends...

It's important for both of you to have friends—jointly and individually. One common mistake many newly married couples make is to think that because their spouse is now their best friend, they may not need any others. If you each had friends before you were married, there should be no reason not to maintain many friendships. Ideally your good friends will become both of your friends.

Friends provide an important support system. They support you, both individually and as a couple. Their different life experiences can offer a fresh perspective on how your life and your marriage are going.

Women and men alike often get a different kind of enjoyment and nourishment from relating to their buddies than they get from their spouses. That is only normal. If you expect your spouse to fulfill *all* your needs for companionship—*all* the time—you may be putting far too much pressure on your marriage. Developing and maintaining friendships, individually and as a couple, allows each of you to grow as individuals. When each of you is stronger, your marriage, in turn, grows stronger.

Developing and maintaining friendships, individually and as a couple, allows each of you to grow as individuals. When each of you is stronger, your marriage, in turn, grows stronger.

...Our Friends

Forging new friendships with other couples who have good marriages can be enormously rewarding. Spending time with other happy couples, watching their relationships grow as yours does, reinforces and strengthens your commitment to each other. Socializing with other couples also expands your interests, bringing out different aspects of your personalities that might not be evident when it's just the two of you. You each get to see each other in a new light, which keeps your relationship fresh and exciting.

Your Children Help You Make New Friends

Once you have children, you will find that they provide wonderful opportunities for making new friends. You may meet other parents in the playground, at the park, or in the course of arranging play dates for the children. What better foundation for a friendship than that you both have in common the people you love most in life—your children. Friendships like these can last for decades, and often include longtime friendships between the children as well.

"When our kids were little, we met several other couples, at a nursery school PTA, who had kids the same age as ours and who had similar interests to ours," says Lilo. "It turned out they had great marriages, too—and they've been our friends for fifty years.

"About ten years ago, when one of our friends was widowed, we all started a picnic club," Gerry continues. "We would meet once a month and have a picnic dinner together—in the park where our kids used to play, or in one of the couples' homes if the weather wasn't good. We added five other couples. Some are widowed now, but we all still meet and feel close, because we know so much about the ups and downs of each other's lives and the lives of all our children."

Celebrate Often with Friends and Family

The happiest couples go out of their way to look for special occasions, both large and small, to celebrate their love and happiness with friends and family They don't just have fun on birthdays, holidays, and anniversaries. They create festive occasions in between—picnics, dinner parties, neighborhood gatherings, family reunions—to get everybody together. In many families, as the relatives get older, they get together for funerals or memorial services It is much better not to wait for a sad occasion, but to look for happy occasions, while everyone is alive and well, to celebrate together.

Give Back to Your Community and the World

The same qualities that make you a good marriage partner make you a good citizen. To be a good marriage partner you have to look beyond your own needs as an individual to the needs of your spouse. To be a good citizen, you have to look beyond your own needs and those of your family to the larger needs of others in the community. Being good in one arena reinforces the other. By making your community a better place to live, you are making yourself just a little bit better, too. That, in turn, will strengthen the bond of your relationship. It is also some of the most deeply satisfying and pleasurable work you can do.

Helping others gives you and your partner another chance to celebrate successes. Building a community pool in your neighborhood, helping children learn to read, bringing a better politician into office, or finding a home for a homeless family gives you great cause to celebrate—and to meet interesting people who share your outlook.

The opportunities to enjoy the satisfaction of serving your community are endless. You can work in a soup kitchen; volunteer to teach at your local school as a teacher's aide or a tutor; organize fund-raisers for a new church, synagogue, or mosque; coach Little League or soccer; or be a Scout leader. You don't have to wait until after retirement to begin! Doing something worthwhile and challenging leaves you feeling better about the world and yourselves. You realize how lucky you are.

Whether you and your partner work together or separately, doing something for others brings out the best in each of you. You have one more thing to admire. That goes double when you can get your children involved, too. Your whole family—grandchildren included—will reap the benefits.

"I was eating lunch with my seven-year-old granddaughter after her riding lesson, when she spilled some Coke on the floor," Gerry, the proud grandfather, recalls. "She went to get paper towels to clean it up. As she wiped up the spill, she realized the floor looked much whiter in that patch than the rest. So she spilled out some more Coke and cleaned a bigger and bigger section of the floor until practically the whole floor was spotless. I said, 'The floor looks nice now, but why did you do it?' She looked at me with a very serious face and said, 'How else can I make the world a better place, Grandpa?'"

You Get Back More Than You Give

Building a happy, healthy life together brings you full circle. The love and respect you've shared with each other become the seeds of love and respect for others. Your ability to share in decision making gives you stability and a sense that you're in it together. Having a wonderful sex life keeps you feeling vibrant and intimately connected. Staying fit and healthy gives you the energy and enthusiasm to experience more fun and more pleasure in your lives.

Nearly every aspect of your lives together is enhanced by a good marriage. You're likely to surround yourself with friends who also have good marriages. You'll have an exciting partner with whom to explore each day. If you're lucky, you'll have the unparalleled joy of raising children together. If you're even luckier and work hard at your marriage all your lives, you may also be able to see your children and grandchildren carry on your tradition and have great marriages for themselves.

"Lilo and I suspected we would be happy together more than five decades ago when we first met, but the reality is even better than our dreams," Gerry says.

"We imagined us together, as a little old couple, holding hands," Lilo adds. Gerry continues Lilo's thought. "We're not just holding hands, we're still dancing, we're still making love, and we're still skiing down mountains together. Looking back, I know we couldn't have had such a great life with anyone else."

"Gerry got me to be more adventurous, and I got him to be more sociable. We have as much fun now as we did when we were younger. Being married has widened our world immeasurably," Lilo says. "We love the spouses of our children, and our grandchildren—our family has been one of the greatest joys. We've shared the magic of a wonderful marriage and the miracle of children. The best part is being there for each other. We also were fortunate to be able to have an impact on our community together. In a great marriage you get older—but not *old*."

A Dating Primer:
A Quick Guide to Online
Sites, Personals, and
Matchmaking Services

I F YOU ARE LOOKING TO MEET AND date new people, you should try as many different avenues as possible. This quick guide covers the ins and outs of dating services and how to make the most of them. These are options that many are using with great success.

Online Dating Sites

The number of dating sites, along with the number of people visiting them—of all ages, backgrounds, and interests—has grown at a staggering rate in the last few years.

More than 45 million Americans visited online dating sites each month in 2004—up from 35 million in 2002. Both the number of visitors as well as the number of sites continues to rise. One of the larger sites, eHarmony, claims that its site yielded 1,500 marriages in its first year of existence, after launching on August 22, 2000. The company's latest figures show that ten couples a day who have met online at their site are now planning weddings—that's well over 3,000 per year.

Services vary in what they offer. Some have listings only. Others include live chat, voice, and video—where you can chat live online with a prospective date and you can also add audio and video messages to your online profile. Most dating sites charge a monthly subscription fee that allows you to communicate with people profiled on the site. Many offer free trial periods before they start charging a monthly service fee.

To multiply your options, there are general interest sites and specialty sites that focus on certain interests or characteristics. The general sites offer the widest range of possibilities, both of the type of person you might encounter and of the sort of encounter that might take place: anonymous e-mail, telephone contact, a serious relationship, or something brief and wild. Special-interest sites cater to a group you may already identify with by religion, race, nationality, age, educational background, hobby—you name it.

Below are some of the major general and specialty online services.

www.match.com

In business since 1995 (a long time in Internet years), Match. com has some interesting wrinkles in its database: subcategories for "anonymous contact" (flirting) by mobile phone, and for finding singles while on vacation. It is part of IAC Interactive Corporation, which also owns the Home Shopping Network. Some subsidiary dating sites (for a youngish demographic) are kiss.com and udate.com. Last year alone, more than 89,000 Match.com members reported they found the person they were seeking.

www.eHarmony.com

In an attempt to eliminate those who do not take matchmaking seriously, this site requires registrants to pass its "emotional readiness" test. Afterward, you can contact only other registrants whose personality traits match your own.

personals.yahoo.com

Yahoo, the Internet giant, casts a vast geographic net, from Ireland to Hong Kong, and, in addition to matchmaking in the United States, offers matchmaking in Spanish in the United States.

www.JDate.com

JDate is for Jewish singles in the United States, Israel, and Europe. Though the company claims this site as the largest network for Jewish singles interested in finding a Jewish partner, many people who are not Jewish also participate.

www.catholicsingles.com

CatholicSingles, a wholly owned Catholic company, is the largest Catholic site and it offer offers weekly advice columns from its staff of clergy and links to Catholic resources.

www.islamicpersonals.com and www.muslimdating.net

These sites feature advice columns on marriage and male/female relations, from an Islamic or Muslim religious perspective.

www.MatchNet.com

MatchNet is a British company with pages that cater to American adults and college students. It was created in 1998 by the founders of jdate.com, a site for Jewish singles.

www.Matchmaker.com

Lycos, not to be outdone by Yahoo, has its own site with worldwide reach. And it's been around for nearly twenty years.

www.premium-dating-services.com

This site is a hub with links to about sixty special-interest sites.

www.goodgenes.com

Goodgenes is a site for the graduates and faculty of Ivy League colleges and other selective schools and universities. The site checks your credentials.

www.rightstuffdating.com and www.squaredating.com

Sites for Ivy League graduates, similar to goodgenes.com.

www.christianoptions.com and www.thebigchurch.com

In addition to bringing Christian singles together, the first site offers daily scripture texts, a weekly devotional page, prayer request page, and Bible quizzes; the second also offers its members Bible study and prayer partners in their hometown or across the world.

Personals

Before online dating existed, many people swore by the personals at the back end of city magazines and local newspapers. These continue to be a great way to meet people who share similar interests, attitudes, and geographical locations.

With personal ads, you get to describe exactly what characteristics you want in a mate and you get a lot of responses in a short time. You can even ask those who respond to describe themselves and include a photo. It's completely up to you whom you respond to or whether you respond to any of them or not. You get to screen people, with no hard feelings on anyone's part.

Because personal ads in magazines and newspapers are so much shorter and less detailed than online profiles, you need as many opportunities for making judgments about respondents as possible. One of the best ways to get to know someone is to hear their voice— through voicemail.

As soon as you place your ad, you should set up your voicemail recording so as not to miss any responses. Take as much care with the content and sound of that recording as you did with the ad. You want to sound relaxed, confident, and appealing. You also have the opportunity to give additional information that you may not have been able to include in the written ad.

Most voicemail recordings allow for two or three minutes—that is as much time as a major news story on the nightly news. You can say a great deal in that length of time. So you will probably want to script out what you plan to say—and practice it until you can say it clearly and naturally.

If you record a detailed message, it will encourage an equally detailed message in return. The more information you can get at this stage, the more comfortable you will feel about who you want to follow up with.

Professional Matchmaking Services

Many people feel they are just too busy to go through the process of writing ads and searching online. Perhaps they are new to town and just don't know where to begin. Or they have tried the other options with no success. If that describes your position, you may be ready for someone to take an active role in screening candidates for you.

There are two kinds of matchmaking services: computer matches and personalized matches. With computer matching services, you fill out a questionnaire and you are matched, by computer, to others who seem to have criteria in common. There is no real human intervention. If the computer dating service has a large data bank of people, and their questionnaires include those criteria that are really important to you, they will be useful in narrowing down the leads for you. Those are big "ifs."

Personalized matching services involve a human being, not just a computer, who interviews you, takes down your answers, and hand-picks possible matches. Some services make a videotape of your in-terview for viewing by other paying clients, so you can also request possible matches with people who look appealing to you.

This type of service can be quite expensive—from a few hun-dred to several thousand dollars (prices are often negotiable). There is never a guarantee of finding you a mate. So be careful and ask questions. Find out if the person doing the interviewing is the same person who will be doing the screening. If not, you will lose the ad-vantage you had of a personal, live interview. If you get passed on to another person in the firm who has never met you, how will they be able to make an appropriate match? Find out how many people in your age range and geographical area they have in their data bank. Find out how many are active members—registered within the last six months (or a year). Get references from satisfied customers.

Composing Your Profile or Ad

Whether you are writing a description of yourself for your local newspaper, city magazine, or online dating service, take some time to read through the other ads to see what format they usually follow and which ads attract your attention.

If you don't know exactly what to say in your ad, start out simply making a list of your own attributes: your personality traits, physical traits, hobbies, family, travel experiences and preferences, religion, sports, exercise, health habits, politics, whatever you think are the most important elements of who you are, what you are proudest of in yourself, and what you would not want to change even for someone you love. Then list what you're looking for in a partner.

Be specific rather than general. Though you may like "walks on the beach," who doesn't? It hardly narrows your search to those candidates who are truly suited to your preferences. You want to narrow your search just enough to eliminate those who would be inappropriate, but not narrow it so much that you may eliminate a possible great partner.

INCLUDE A PHOTO, OR HAVE ONE READY TO SEND OUT

We are all looking for that special chemistry, and though a photo is not as foolproof as in-person contact, it can give you an important additional clue as to how well-suited you might be for each other.

If you're going the online route, get a friend who has a good eye and a digital camera to snap shots of you in happy, natural poses. Pick two or three of the best and upload them along with your profile. As you might expect, profiles with photos get the best response online.

If you are using the personal ads, have a photo ready to send out to potential dates you've contacted, in response to someone else's ad. To avoid divulging your home address, you can take out a post office box and use that for the duration of your ads.

EVALUATING YOUR RESPONSES

Read the written and e-mail responses you get over and over. Do the same with the voicemail messages you get. Consider the tone as well as the words. Bear in mind that many people include "small deceptions." Men often add an inch or two to their height; women tend to be "slender," whether they are or not. Both sexes may alter their residences to make it seem as if they live in a more affluent or hip place than they actually do. But in the end, trust your initial instincts about whether they sound appealing.

Take notes on each response and keep detailed records. You won't be able to remember them all. Start e-mailing. When you're ready to go to the next step, pick up the phone.

TIPS ON MAKING THE INITIAL CONTACT

When you call the first time, try calling at a time of day when you think the person might not be at home. It will give you the opportunity to listen to the voicemail message, which can be as informative as the response they left for your ad. Call at a time when you can focus 100 percent of your attention on the conversation, without interruptions from roommates, neighbors, dogs, children, or anything else.

When you do connect on the phone, do not rush into setting up a date. Ask all your questions and try to get to know the person. Don't be afraid to get personal. Talking on the phone is a further screening tool to see if you really have enough in common to go out on a date. It is usually best to talk on the phone more than once—you want to have a good sense of who they are, what their intentions are, and whether they seem right for you.

FIRST DATES

Once you decide you have enough in common with someone to actually meet for a date in person, make the first meeting in a public place. Always provide your own transportation. Make the date simple, inexpensive, casual. Meet for a cup of coffee or an ice cream cone. If you do not hit it off, at least you have not committed yourself to spending an entire evening and a lot of money on a dinner with someone you never want to see again.

On the other hand, if things go wonderfully, you can always extend the date. Or better yet, arrange a follow-up on another day for a longer adventure. It may be the beginning of a wonderful relationship.

A Wellness Primer:
Seven Rules
for Staying Healthy

H ERE ARE SEVEN SIMPLE RULES FOR STAYING healthy in mind, body, and spirit. If you have any questions about your physical or emotional health, make sure you consult with a professional health care provider.

1. Eat a Healthy Diet

Canyon Ranch, the highly regarded health and fitness resort based in Tucson, Arizona, has elevated healthy eating to an art because they know that if food isn't delicious as well as nutritious, nobody will eat it for long. Their diet guidelines are presented in *The Canyon Ranch Guide to Living Younger Longer*, which is a wonderful introduction to their philosophy. If you incorporate some of these habits into your day, you will be surprised at how quickly you begin to feel the positive effects.

GET TO YOUR OPTIMAL WEIGHT

Are you at your optimal weight? If not, is your goal to lose weight, as it is for more than one-fourth of the population in the United States that is overweight? If so, pay special attention to these two tips from the National Weight Control Registry, which tracks the progress and experiences of thousands of successful dieters: *exercise every day* and *cut back on your consumption of problem foods*—those high-fat and high-carbohydrate foods that are so easy to go overboard in eating, such as junk food, tortilla chips, ice cream, cookies, and alcohol.

165

EAT REGULARLY

Healthy eaters and successful dieters do not skip breakfast or other meals. Eating smaller meals every three to five hours throughout the day has been shown to be the healthiest pattern for preventing over-eating and fatigue, sustaining optimal energy, and losing weight. Or you can have a small snack in the late afternoon so that you are not ravenous at dinnertime.

BE MINDFUL OF PORTION SIZES

Excessively large portion sizes can sabotage anyone's healthy diet. The super-sized meals at most restaurants contain more calories and fat than most people need to eat in a day, let alone a meal. The best guide is to stick to portions the size of your own palm or a deck of playing cards.

EAT EIGHT TO TEN SERVINGS OF FRUIT AND VEGETABLES A DAY

The most nutritious fruits tend to be the most colorful—red, blue, orange, yellow. The best vegetables are the dark green variety (asparagus, broccoli, kale, romaine, spinach), as well as the dark purples and red (eggplant, cabbage).

EMPHASIZE WHOLE GRAINS AND FIBER

Whole grains and fiber keep your blood sugar levels stable, so you don't get as hungry between meals. Complex carbohydrates are better than simple ones, as they provide essential nutrients and do not break down into sugars as quickly. They include such foods as beans, barley, brown rice, wild rice, whole wheat, bran and multigrain breads and cereals, soybeans, nuts, and seeds.

FOCUS ON HEALTHY FATS AND OILS

Fat should constitute no more than 20 to 30 percent of your daily calories. *The healthiest are the vegetable oils, such as olive, canola, and grape seed oils*, high in mono-saturated fats. Fish oils are great sources of omega-3 fatty acids, anti-inflammatory agents that benefit all tissues, from the lining of blood vessels to the brain cells. *Avoid the saturated (solid) fats* in butter and animal products, as well as solid oils such as shortening and margarine that are ingredients in many snack foods and used to fry many fast food dishes.

BALANCE EACH MEAL WITH SOME PROTEIN-RICH FOOD

Many Americans overload on protein, but if you only have small protein portions throughout the day, you can keep your energy levels even and avoid getting so hungry that you will be tempted to over-eat. Red meat is not the only protein source. Chicken, fish, and soy products are good low-fat proteins. Beans and rice, eaten together, form a complete and low-fat protein.

LIMIT THE AMOUNT OF SUGAR IN YOUR DIET—AVOID ARTIFICIAL SWEETENERS

Americans tend to overdose on sweets, consuming on average twenty teaspoons a day. Artificial sweeteners can make sugar cravings even worse. The best bet is to substitute natural sweeteners for sugar when possible, such as fruit juice and maple syrup.

BE SENSIBLE ABOUT SALT

Too much salt can be a problem, especially if you have high blood pressure or other heart-related disorders. You do not need to sacrifice flavor, if you experiment with garlic, lemon juice, ginger, and herbs and spices as you reduce the salt. Avoid processed food and frozen meals that are often very high in sodium.

DRINK PLENTY OF WATER

It shouldn't be surprising that we need plenty of water—the human body is almost two-thirds water. Most nutritionists suggest you consume eight glasses a day. Watch out for alcohol and caffeinated drinks—these take away more water than they replenish.

2. Get Enough Sleep

If you want to wake up in the morning looking forward to a brand-new day, it helps to get the sleep your body needs. *Most people function best on seven to nine hours of sleep.* Though there are many famous individuals who boasted that they could get by on less—President Lyndon Johnson claimed to need only four, as did Napoleon, Thomas Edison, and artist Salvador Dali—most people experience impaired mental and physical acuity on such little rest.

Tiredness can make you more prone to accidents—and fights with your spouse. It can interfere with job performance. Being well-rested can make you much better company—and it can do wonders for your love life.

Disruptions in sleep patterns can indicate a health problem. If you are having trouble sleeping over a long period of time, or you find yourself falling asleep during the day, it is worth consulting your doctor. You may need to be checked for sleep apnea, depression, or other common disorders. There are excellent treatments available and you will be glad you got help.

If you find yourself unable to get your usual rest for just a few nights, because of deadlines or stress and worry, take comfort in the resiliency of the human body. No matter how much sleep you have lost, you can make up for it—and feel back to normal—after only a couple of nights of normal sleep.

To avoid the most common sleep problems, here are some techniques to try.

- Limit caffeine intake over the course of the day—it can have a cumulative effect. Do not consume any caffeine within seven hours of when you aim to fall asleep that night.
- Don't exercise late at night. Such exertion can stimulate you instead of making you tired and ready for bed.
- Time your evening meal carefully. If you are on a diet, you may have discovered it is almost as hard to fall asleep on an empty stomach as on a full one. Don't eat a big dinner too close to bedtime. But save enough calories in your daily allotment to have a small bedtime snack so you feel calm, drowsy, and ready for sleep.
- Avoid naps if you are having sleep problems, at least until you get back on your regular sleep schedule.
- Clear your mind of all thoughts and focus solely on taking deep, steady, calming breaths. Repeat until you feel relaxed and sleepy.

- Good sex is one of the best sleep aids nature ever invented. Sweet dreams.

3. Exercise Regularly

Regular exercise, every day, if possible, makes you look great and feel great. Getting fit—for yourself and your spouse—can do wonderful things for your relationship. Exercise improves your mood, your sleep, and your self-esteem, all of which makes you more fun to be with. And it has been shown to improve memory and brain function.

Exercise is also a wonderful way to reduce stress, relieve anxiety, and just relax. That promotes better sleep...and more. When you feel fit, and know you look fit, there is nothing better to put you in the mood for romance.

The best exercise is the exercise you love doing—because that is what you will keep on doing. To get the most out of exercise, you need to come up with a routine that you engage in several times a week. Your aim should be to cover all the bases: cardiovascular fitness, strength, flexibility, and balance.

Consider joining a gym and getting a good trainer to show you what exercises to do and how to use the machines safely. Buy exercise tapes to do at home. Join a neighborhood pick-up game. Take a stroll after dinner with your partner—and the children; it aids digestion and restores both calm and energy as you face the evening. Walk or ride a bike instead of driving. Find some walking or jogging partners. Then put exercise in your schedule at least three hours a week, either a half hour six days or an hour three times a week. You'll be glad you did.

INCREASE YOUR CARDIOVASCULAR FITNESS

Aerobic exercise gets your heart pumping, improves blood circulation and the body's ability to use oxygen, provides energy, and raises the levels of good cholesterol (HDLs or high-density lipoproteins) in your blood. Best of all, aerobics improve your mood. An intensive aerobic workout stimulates your body's productions of endorphins, the chemicals that produce what is often referred to as the "runner's high" and make you feel great.

A RELAXING DEEP-BREATHING EXERCISE

Lie on the floor or on your bed. Watch your stomach rise and fall as you breathe in and out. Focus on how the air feels: cool as it flows in, hot as it flows out. Now take three deep breaths, and put all thoughts out of your mind except the cool air flowing in, the hot air flowing out, as you inhale and exhale slowly. With each breath you should feel more and more relaxed.

DON'T FORGET STRENGTH TRAINING

Increasing your musculature improves your coordination, builds bone density, eases such chronic problems as back pain and arthritis, and increases lean body mass, which helps you manage your weight. All you need are a few dumbbells or weights and you can do the lifting right at home.

BEGIN AND END WITH STRETCHING

Begin and end your day—as well as your exercise sessions—with gentle stretching. It keeps you supple, improves your posture, and helps you maintain your sense of balance so you can be free to dance, garden, or just have fun with your partner.

4. Make Time for Recreational Activities

Engaging in leisure activities—especially active ones like sports—gives a great boost to your mind and your body.

Evelyn and Gary, married thirty-two years, have always made their free time count.

"We did a lot of backpacking and camping when we were younger," recalls Evelyn. "We still take hikes, and have added cross-country skiing. We feel like kids again. It reminds us that we're still young at heart even though our children are fully grown. We've recently joined a health club. We'll meet at the club, work out in the gym for a couple of hours, and then go home together for a nice dinner. It's the complete date."

5. *Don't Smoke or Abuse Alcohol or Prescription Drugs*

The first part sounds easy. Don't smoke. There is no gray area. No amount of smoking can be good for you. So if you are smoking, quit. If you aren't, don't start. It will shorten your life, and that's not fair to your partner.

Alcohol and prescription drugs pose slightly trickier dilemmas. In moderation, these substances can be helpful and even enhance your life and health. However, it is all too easy to move from moderation to the trouble zone. If you suspect that one of you has made that move—or your spouse voices even the slightest concern that you are not using alcohol or prescription drugs appropriately—take that as a sign to cut your consumption back immediately. If you find it hard to stop, seek professional help or join a support group.

6. *Be Positive—Optimists Live Longer*

Developing a positive mental attitude is critical to maintaining optimum health. Happy couples avoid criticism and look at the world and each other with a positive slant.

Optimism also keeps you healthier, according to research conducted by the Mayo Clinic in Rochester, Minnesota. Optimists live longer than pessimists. They also do not get sick as often, according to other research at the University of Minnesota. When they do get sick, they recover more quickly.

Being positive is a daily habit you can cultivate. Remind yourself to focus on what is right about your lover, your marriage, and the world around you instead of complaining about everything that is wrong. Start by being nice to yourself as well as everyone you see during the day. When you can accept yourself as you are, flaws and all, you will find it much easier to accept the people you love.

7. *Reduce Stress and Relax*

There are plenty of good reasons for couples to try to reduce the stress in their lives. It's hard to be as loving and caring as you like to be when you're under stress. Few people find themselves in the mood for romance and sex when they are stressed out. And, of course, stress

LOOK FOR THE FUNNY SIDE

Get in the habit of looking for even one small thing in the midst of a stressful situation that you can feel appreciative about—or better yet, that you can see as even the slightest bit funny. It will remove you enough from the tension at hand to let you step back, rethink what you are going through, and, after a few deep breaths, enable you to relax.

Rent a funny movie and laugh as loud as you can without startling the neighbors. Did you know that children laugh twenty-seven times as often as adults? Why should they have all the fun? You can't be mad or depressed when you laugh. So let loose, let go, laugh, and feel better.

does untold damage to your mind and body. Chronic stress is associated with nearly every health problem you can name, from asthma, cancer, and diabetes to headaches, heart disease, and ulcers.

Regular physical exercise is one way to reduce stress. More and more people are also turning to yoga, a 5,000-year-old system of postures and breathing, as a powerful tool for combating stress and achieving calm. It has become so popular that you can find yoga classes in nearly every health club; it is even being taught to children in dozens of schools across the country. By using controlled breathing as you carry out a series of carefully executed body poses, yoga aims to increase strength, endurance, and stamina while bringing the dual forces of the mind and body into balance.

Deep breathing and other meditation practices are also enormously helpful in enhancing our sense of equilibrium. Most of us take our breathing for granted. But the depth and pace of our breathing can have a powerful influence over our moods, our ability to focus, and the level of stress we feel. Simply slowing your breathing—without doing any other thing—will immediately make you feel more relaxed.

T E R R E N C E   R E A L

Proven Techniques
for a Wonderful Marriage

We must become the change we wish for in the world.

—MAHATMA GANDHI

GREAT RELATIONSHIPS ARE NOT CREATED BY MAGIC. As the Leeds have noted, and my practice has continually demonstrated, great relationships are a product of attention and ongoing practice. I'm delighted to be part of this book because it provides a wise, straightforward road map to a great marriage, written by two people with more than fifty years of experience in their own wonderful marriage.

Five Techniques for Great Relationships

Based on my observations of literally hundreds of couples, I've pulled together five techniques that couples in great marriages demonstrate time and time again. No one is perfect, and every couple has conflict. In great relationships, couples have learned how to work through conflict in a way that enhances and deepens the relationship. In great relationships, couples have learned how to get their needs met, and how to meet the needs of their partners. The five techniques below can help you improve the quality of your relationship:

1. Speak Out with Love and Savvy—speak your mind thoughtfully and with love.
2. Respond with Generosity—remember you are speaking to someone you love.
3. Empower Each Other—communicate in a way that inspires positive action.
4. Ask for What You Need—don't complain about what's wrong.
5. Cherish Each Other—make the time and space to truly enjoy each other.

1. Speak Out with Love and Savvy

Every relationship, no matter how strong, has conflicts. Great relationships don't avoid conflicts but, rather, handle them with love and kindness. Of course, we are only human and when we feel hurt our first reactions may not be loving or considerate. Even though we rationally know that words spoken in anger can create more distance between partners, we may want to retaliate, saying something that will hurt our partner's feelings just as our feelings were hurt. Or we may just want to withdraw, to pull away from our partner in a way that protects ourselves and makes our partner feel bad for the hurt he or she has caused.

Both of these responses, retaliation and withdrawal, are what I call "losing strategies" and can actually provoke a partner even more. Instead of retaliating or withdrawing, partners should speak up, but thoughtfully, and with love.

Another losing strategy is unbridled self-expression. Some couples seem to have the mistaken idea that intimacy means saying anything and everything that comes into one's mind. Successful couples think before they speak and consider how their partner will feel about it. They recognize that some thoughts should go unvoiced.

DON'T YIELD TO YOUR FIRST REACTION

Before you act, ask yourself whether this action will help you achieve your goals. Will it get you what you want? Will it help forge a stronger bond with your partner? Are your words kind? If the answer is no, then stop and reconsider.

In that moment you must call upon a less reactive, more mature part of you, the part that says, *Hold it, breathe! You know what going through that door will get you. This time let's try a new door. This time, for example, let's not fight; let's speak moderately. This time, let's not avoid; let's deal with the issue without blaming or criticizing.* It can be hard not to yield to your first impulse, but it gets easier with practice. With practice, you'll get better at avoiding that knee-jerk, unhelpful reaction and replacing it with one that builds love and trust. You can learn to pause, breathe, and reach for a saner, more loving response. It is the voice of our adult self. In great relationships each partner deliberately and consistently listens to that voice.

And here's the great news. As we attend to it, the relationship grows stronger. Every time we choose a smart action over a dumb one, we build our relationship muscles, until smart actions begin to be the norm, and self-defeating reactions become the exception. No matter how miserable, or nasty, or frightened your exchanges have been, you can change your patterns. Never stop working on communicating better with your partner. By working and practicing healthy and loving communication you can get beyond your habitual response and make yourself try something better. As the Leeds advise you to be more patient in your relationship and control your knee-jerk response, they call upon you here, and throughout the book, to be *conscious of your actions,* to deliberately choose a more thoughtful, more loving response.

Chances are you'll be rewarded for it—thoughtful, savvy choices work. And you'll get better at it as you build your relational muscles. Like any other practice, though, the work is in the doing. You can gain insight, or vent feelings all day long, but nothing will change until you make the decision to change your behavior. So get going—even if you do it badly at first. Start where you can and build on it.

2. *Respond with Generosity*

In great relationships, partners respond to each other with kindness and generosity. The first step is to be willing to simply listen to your partner, as listening is one of the most loving things we can do for our partner.

It's very natural for a couple to try to resolve their differences by eliminating them. Faced with conflicting views, it's natural to believe the way to eliminate the conflict is to figure out who is right (or, more to the point, to convince your partner that your view is the correct one). It's natural, but it's wrong. Your goal should never be to win an argument but instead it should be to work toward a solution that makes you *both* happy. It's time to embrace a radical idea—it doesn't matter who is right. What matters is the relationship.

LET GO OF BEING RIGHT

The next time you find yourself arguing, remind yourself that it really doesn't matter who is right. What matters is resolving the conflict with love and generosity. As the Leeds say, "being kind is more important that being right."

Overwhelmingly, our approach to dealing with problems is through discussion: you tell me your side and I'll tell you mine, and we'll work it out. In many cases this can work just fine. But in some cases this approach simply won't work. Have you ever had an argument that seems to last for years, going through various permutations each time? Discussion of a highly charged issue that follows the pattern of *that's your side, here's my side*, only increases tension because neither side feels sufficiently heard or understood. In a great relationship both you and your partner can, if you must, air that you're upset about an issue, *but not at the same time*.

While your partner may be too polite to say it, someone experiencing distress, no matter how intent on making things right, isn't really interested in your thoughts, your feelings, or your reasons or explanations. In that moment, your partner really isn't focusing on you at all. What he or she needs to know is whether or not you care.

JUST LISTEN

In an argument, instead of focusing on getting your views understood, decide, for now, that you will focus on understanding your partner's perspective and putting yourself in his or her shoes. Let your partner speak his or her mind, and don't interrupt, even if he or she is getting the facts wrong, misinterpreting your motives, or misunderstanding the situation. Your goal is to understand your partner, not correct him or her. You don't have to agree; you just have to understand that this is how your partner sees it.

Repeat it back to your partner. "So you feel that . . ." Make sure he or she understands that you get it, that you hear and appreciate what he is saying. By asking questions and verbally acknowledging you understand your partner's point of view, you will make him or her feel heard and validated.

Once you have demonstrated that you do care and love your partner, then he or she can begin to focus on your perspective. But before that occurs, the distressed partner will inevitably perceive any attempt to focus on your experience as a deflection of the issue. And though you may have nothing but the best of intentions, your partner will see your behavior as defensive, selfish, or evasive.

Listening is important, but it's not enough. You must then respond with generosity. Once you've listened, and acknowledged your partner's perspective, you should grant as many of your partner's requests as you can. In healthy relationships, no one has anything to prove. If you find yourself unwilling to grant a request, is it because your partner has asked for something unreasonable? Or is it because you don't want to be told what to do? Try not to resist for childish reasons, and instead be generous, remembering that your generosity is the most powerful way to instill generosity in your partner.

3. Empower Each Other

If you want the best from your partner, you need to treat him or her in a way that inspires a positive response to your requests. The first step is to ask for what you want. I have a saying: *You don't have the*

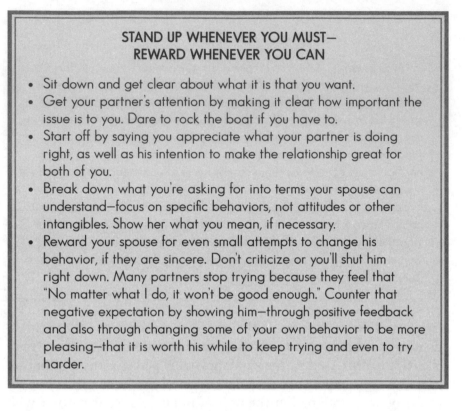

STAND UP WHENEVER YOU MUST— REWARD WHENEVER YOU CAN

- Sit down and get clear about what it is that you want.
- Get your partner's attention by making it clear how important the issue is to you. Dare to rock the boat if you have to.
- Start off by saying you appreciate what your partner is doing right, as well as his intention to make the relationship great for both of you.
- Break down what you're asking for into terms your spouse can understand—focus on specific behaviors, not attitudes or other intangibles. Show her what you mean, if necessary.
- Reward your spouse for even small attempts to change his behavior, if they are sincere. Don't criticize or you'll shut him right down. Many partners stop trying because they feel that "No matter what I do, it won't be good enough." Counter that negative expectation by showing him—through positive feedback and also through changing some of your own behavior to be more pleasing—that it is worth his while to keep trying and even to try harder.

right to get mad about not getting what you never asked for. This is particularly germane for women still laboring under the romantic ideal that "If I have to ask for it, it doesn't count." Sorry, girls. Cinderella's dead and Prince Charming probably just got out of rehab. In today's world, you have to do the hard work.

4. Ask for What You Need—Don't Complain about What's Wrong

You might think that in these modern, enlightened times, men and women would have finally learned how to identify their desires and assert them. But you'd be wrong. Even in good relationships, many men and women seem to subscribe to the truly nutty idea that the way to get what you want from your partner is *to complain about it after the fact.* Perhaps you believe that your request will be denied or that

---

CHANGE THE WAY YOU ASK

It's easy to complain, especially when you're irritated by your partner's behavior and you really feel in the right. But it's not effective. Instead of complaining, take a breath, calm yourself, remember that this is someone you love, and ask for what you want clearly and without negativity or criticism.

Instead of saying:
   "David, I can't believe you never get home in time to help with the kids. There are three of them and it's just too much for me to deal with supper and homework for all of them every night. Don't you have any consideration?"

Try saying:
   "David, I'm finding it overwhelming to deal with the three kids on my own each night. I really need you to help me with this; it's very important to me. Do you think you can find a way to get home by six at least three nights a week?"

---

your partner should magically know your needs, so you don't clearly or specifically verbalize what you need. In many instances complaining feels safer than the risk of being turned down or rejected. But, in reality, complaining about what your partner did wrong rarely changes behavior. Your partner may feel bad, he or she may even apologize, but rarely will he or she start doing things differently.

Making this shift can be hard for some couples. It's easy to complain; you aren't taking any risks. When you ask for what you want, there's a risk your partner will say no, or say yes, but then disappoint you. But in great relationships each partner feels that his or her needs are important and that it's acceptable to ask for what you want.

5. Cherish Each Other

The four winning strategies I discuss above focus on techniques for setting things right and getting the most from you relationship with your partner. The final winning strategy, cherishing, focuses on what

179

SHOW YOUR APPRECIATION

Show your appreciation. At the end of each day, tell your partner at least one thing you appreciate about him or her, either about something that happened that day, or something long-standing. "I really appreciate your listening to me earlier this evening" or "You have always had the most beautiful eyes." Remember saying things like that? This can and should continue throughout your relationship. Appreciate little things; they don't have to be monumental. Write notes telling your partner something positive about his or her behavior that matters to you. Leave a message or an e-mail. If you do this, day in and day out, you will nurture your great relationship and keep it strong. Appreciating your partner will also encourage her to reciprocate the positivity and it will forge a pattern of kindness and appreciation, from *both* partners.

to do when things are going well, when you are living the wonderful marriage. Building a great relationship takes skill, and it also takes skill to cherish having it and keep it well.

You may be thinking, *Well, I certainly don't have that problem*, but I advise you to think this over carefully. You may be right, but if so, you are a rare individual. It's only too easy for couples in a good relationship to take each other for granted, and to focus more on what they want from their partners than appreciating what they have. Also, it's easier to appreciate one another if you are living a happy life *together*: have date nights, take a vacation as a couple, cultivate shared interests and hobbies, spend quality time without children or other family and friends, and remember that when you focus on the fun you have together, it's easier to appreciate one another.

I believe that the winning strategy of cherishing is as important as the other four put together, and it's easy to do once it becomes part of the way you think about your relationship and your partner. As the Leeds say, it's simply a matter of always wanting to give your partner the best strawberries.

Recommended Reading: Some Favorite Books to Help Make Your Relationship Great

Ten Elements of a Great Marriage

The Case for Marriage: Why Married People Are Happier, Healthier, and Better Off Financially. Linda J. Waite and Maggie Gallagher. New York: Doubleday, 2000.

There is an excellent mix of original and historical research data on why marriage is such an important and beneficial institution. If you were not convinced of the advantages of marriage before, you will be after.

The Dance of Intimacy: A Woman's Guide to Courageous Acts of Change in Key Relationships. Harriet Lerner, Ph.D. New York: Harper & Row, 1989.

Lerner discusses how to navigate between the essential separateness and connectedness that leads to genuine intimacy in relationships.

The Exceptional Seven Percent: The Nine Secrets of The World's Happiest Couples. Gregory K. Popcak, MSW. New York: Citadel Press Books, 2000.

The author outlines what exceptionally happy couples have in common. Within that estimated seven percent of exceptionally happy couples, there are a variety of different kinds of marriages and partnerships possible.

1. Get Yourself Ready

Emotional Intelligence. David Goleman. New York: Bantam Books, 1997.

A science writer and psychologist summarizes recent psychological work and suggests ways to regulate negative emotions through science-based understanding of the self.

Finding Your Own North Star: Claiming the Life You Were Meant to Live. Martha Beck. New York: Crown Publishing Group, 2002.

The author outlines a process of returning to the time when you were the hero of your own life, and, starting again from there, finding one's promised land.

Life Strategies: Doing What Works, Doing What Matters. Phillip C. McGraw, Ph.D. New York: Hyperion Press, 1999.

This hard-nosed book says strategy, not therapy, is needed to get through life's tough problems: face who you really are, name your choices, and plot your way through them.

Living a Life That Matters. Harold S. Kushner. New York: Anchor, 2002.

A rabbi explains that at the heart of self-fulfillment is selflessness—the struggle to overcome the many forms of self-vindication and to play the supporting role that makes other people stars.

Man's Search for Meaning. Viktor Frankl. New York: Washington Square Press, 1997.

First published in 1957, this story of how a psychiatrist survived three years in Nazi concentration camps stands Nietzsche's philosophy of "will to power" on its head. Describing the psychology of survival, the author argues that humans are motivated by the "will to meaning"—the way for each of us to achieve wholeness and dignity.

The Power of Myth. Joseph Campbell, Bill Moyers. New York: Doubleday, 1988.

In conversations transcribed from a six-part TV series for PBS, Campbell explains how the eternal questions in our daily lives—who are we? how can we be fulfilled?—are played out for us in myths. Campbell shows us how our own stories live in those of our mythic heroes.

The Power of Now. Eckhart Tolle. New York: New World Library, 2001.

Instruction on the technique of watching your thoughts in order to find the peace of pure consciousness of the present. An introduction to the art of continual meditation.

Self Reliance and Other Essays. Ralph Waldo Emerson. New York: Dover Publications, 1993.

Emerson wrote 150 years ago that each of us can, and must, quietly and vigorously discover what we are about. When we do that, we can then achieve fulfillment and find our destiny.

2. Date with Purpose

Before You Say "I Do": Important Questions for Couples to Ask Before Marriage. Todd Outcalt. New York: Berkley Publishing Group, 1998.

This book details many of the questions partners should ask to get to know each other better and make sure they are well suited to a lifetime together.

The Committed Marriage: A Guide to Finding a Soul Mate and Building a Relationship Through Timeless Biblical Wisdom. Rebbetzin Esther Jungreis. San Francisco: HarperSanFrancisco, 2002.

Jungreis draws from the Old Testament and her own wisdom, as the wife of a rabbi and the daughter of a long line of rabbis, to guide couples in their search for the right partner and a lasting marriage.

He's Scared, She's Scared. Steven Carter, Julie Sokol. New York: Dell, 1995.

Women balk at commitment, too, and this book addresses their fears and concerns and how to allay them.

If the Buddha Dated. Charlotte Kasl, Ph.D. New York: Penguin Compass, 1999.

How a mind at peace finds—and attracts—a like-minded mate.

3. Put Love and Respect First: Love Poems to Inspire You

Love Letter: An Anthology of Passion. Michelle Lovric. New York: Barnes & Noble, 2003.

In a beautifully printed edition, this book contains an array of facsimiles of real letters and quotations from lovers' correspondence throughout the ages.

Love Poems. Selected and edited by Peter Washington. Everyman's Library. New York: Alfred A. Knopf, 1993.

A lovely collection that takes you through several centuries, from John Donne to e.e. cummings with stops at W. H. Auden and Emily Dickenson in between. The poems deal with the definitions of love, fidelity and inconstancy, estrangement and praising the loved one, and the pleasures and the pains that only love can bring.

Love Poems from God. Translated by Daniel Ladinsky. New York: Penguin Compass, 2002.

Ladinsky, best known for his translations of the great Sufi poet Hafiz, brings together six spiritual writers from the East and six from the West, including Rumi's ecstatic love poems, Saint Francis, and Kabir.

The 100 Best Love Poems of All Time. Edited by Leslie Pockell. New York: Warner Books, 2003.

From old classics, like Shakespeare's "Shall I compare thee to a summer's day," and Edgar Allan Poe's "To Helen" to some newer classics including Theodore Roethke's "I knew a woman," and Sylvia Plath's "Love Letter," this collection has a poem for every lover's heart.

Proposing on the Brooklyn Bridge: Poems About Marriage. Collected by Ginny Lowe Connors. West Hartford, CT: Poetworks/Grayson Books, 2003.

Poems by mostly modern poets, both well-known (Wendell Berry and Richard Wilbur) and lesser-known, about coming together, feeling apart, weddings, anniversaries, and the shape of married life.

Sonnets from the Portuguese: A Celebration of Love. Elizabeth Barrett Browning. New York: St. Martin's Press, 1986.

Browning wrote these forty-four sonnets to her husband, the writer Robert Browning, to celebrate their marriage and their love. He called her his "little Portuguese," and she, in turn, created these love poems that include the classic "How do I love thee? Let me count the ways."

4. Agree on the Big Six

The Antidepressant Survival Guide: The Clinically Proven Program to Enhance the Benefits and Beat the Side Effects of Your Medication. Robert J. Hedaya, M.D. New York: Three Rivers Press, 2000.

There is much useful advice here on how to handle depression, which has become one of the most common emotional and psychological problems in the United States.

The Couple's Guide to Love and Money. Jonathan Rich. Oakland, CA: New Harbinger Publications, 2003.

This practical guide shows partners how to avoid finance-based conflicts and make negotiating money matters both pleasurable and productive. It offers active steps to help couples achieve strong psychological insights into their own money personalities, navigate those differences, and improve communications around this hot-button issue.

The Emotionally Abusive Relationship: How to Stop Being Abused and How to Stop Abusing. Beverly Engel. New York: Wiley, 2002.

According to therapist Engel, "even the most loving person" is capable of emotional abuse—that is, "any nonphysical behavior that is designed to control, intimidate, subjugate, demean, punish, or isolate." In a reasoned, sensible tone, she encourages readers to become responsible for their behavior and for changing it.

The Family CFO: The Couple's Business Plan for Love and Money. Mary Claire Allvine, Christine Larson. Emmaus, PA: Rodale Press, 2004.

Starting with the surprising but sensible idea that households should operate like corporations, certified financial planner Allvine and journalist Larson provide simple and fast rules for couples to effectively merge and manage their assets and liabilities. Only then can they "avoid arguments and anxiety and achieve not just their financial goals but their life goals together."

The Instinct to Heal: Curing Stress, Anxiety, and Depression Without Drugs and Without Talk Therapy. David Servan-Schreiber, M.D., Ph.D. Emmaus, PA: Rodale Press, 2001.

A psychiatrist and cofounder of the University of Pittsburgh's Center for Complementary Medicine, the author prescribes an integrated therapy of nutrition and improved interpersonal communication, in order to free the brain's natural tendencies to heal itself.

Mixed Blessings: Marriage Between Jews and Christians. Paul Cowan and Rachel Cowan. New York: Doubleday, 1987.

Using their own mixed marriage as a starting point, the authors offer advice to couples contemplating a mixed marriage on how to avoid "time bombs" and bring interfaith couples closer.

5. Decide about Marriage

The Knot Guide to Wedding Vows and Traditions: Readings, Rituals, Music, Dances, and Toasts. Carley Roney. New York: Broadway Books, 2000.

Of the dozens of books on wedding planning, this contains one of the more comprehensive selections of vows. The author runs a wedding-planning Web site, www.theknot.com, on which many of the vows are also available.

Words for the Wedding: Creative Ideas for Choosing and Using Hundreds of Quotations to Personalize Your Vows, Toasts, Invitations, and More. Wendy Paris and Andrew Chesler. New York: Berkeley Publishing Group, 2001.

This book offers many alternatives on the wording of vows, organizing its suggestions as variations for each of the sentiments expressed in the most commonly known lines: "for better or for worse," "in sickness and in health," for richer and for poorer," etc.

6. Communicate Lovingly

The Dance of Anger: A Woman's Guide to Changing the Patterns of In-
timate Relationships. Harriet Lerner, Ph. D. New York: Harper &
Row, 1985.

Psychologist Lerner helps women pay attention to the anger
they may feel, understand it, and transform those feelings in a way
that allows each partner, and the relationship, to grow.

Love Is Never Enough: How Couples Can Overcome Misunderstand-
ings, Resolve Conflicts, and Solve Relationship Problems Through
Cognitive Therapy. Aaron T. Beck, M.D. New York: Harper &
Row, 1988.

Beck, a psychiatry professor, focuses on how couples can keep
negative thinking from getting in the way of understanding and
being happy with each other.

Men Are from Mars, Women Are from Venus: A Practical Guide for Im-
proving Communication and Getting What You Want in Your Rela-
tionships. John Gray, Ph.D. New York: HarperCollins, 1992.

In what has now become a classic, Gray explains the fundamental differences between how men and women communicate—and
how they can bridge the inevitable communication gaps. The title
for Chapter 3 summarizes one of the biggest lessons each gender
has to learn about the other: "Men Go to Their Caves and Wom-
en Talk."

People Skills. Robert Bolton, Ph.D. New York: Touchstone Books,
1986.

A user's manual for communication, with specifics on how to
surmount barriers such as defensiveness and aggressiveness.

The Seven Principles for Making Marriage Work. John M. Gottman,
Ph.D., and Nan Silver. New York: Crown Publishers, 1999.

Gottman offers seven guidelines along with detailed questionnaires and exercises for couples to learn how to handle conflict,
solve problems, and grow closer.

7. Make Sex Great for Both of You

*The Art of Sexual Ecstasy: The Path of Sacred Sexuality for West-
ern Lovers.* Margo Anand. New York: Jeremy P. Tarcher/Putnam,
1989.

Summoning ancient Tantric and Taoist techniques, the author
guides Western lovers toward enhanced pleasure and deeper intimacy. As couples become more comfortable with each other and
their sexuality, they find they can expand their orgasmic capabili-
ties and deepen love.

*Guide to Getting It On: The Universe's Coolest and Most Informa-
tive Book about Sex, for Adults of All Ages.* 4th ed. Paul Joannides.
Waldport, OR: Goofy Foot Press, 2004.

This practical, sometimes irreverent, and very explicit guide offers a wide range of information and illustrations on everything
from anatomy, techniques, and fantasies to sex laws in the United
States and explaining sex to children.

New Joy of Sex. Alex Comfort. New York: Pocket Books, 1992.

The illustrated classic, updated with information about safe sex
and other modernisms. In its day the title alone was shocking.

New Male Sexuality, The. rev. ed. Bernie Zilbergeld. New York: Bantam Books, 1999.

The classic book on male sexuality. Here, good sex is defined
as feeling good about yourself, good about your partner, and good
about what you're doing with an emphasis on "pleasure, closeness, and self- and partner-enhancement."

*Passionate Marriage: Keeping Love and Intimacy Alive in Committed
Relationships.* David Schnarch, Ph.D. New York: Henry Holt &
Co., 1998.

A sex and marriage therapist interweaves his advice with the
voices of couples he has counseled to show how they can break
through the blocks that hold them achieving true intimacy and
eroticism in a loving and passionate marriage.

Sex for Dummies. Ruth Westheimer. New York: John Wiley & Sons, Inc., 2000.

A dumb title for a book packed with technical information about sex and desire, in Westheimer's trademark matter-of-fact style.

Sex-Starved Marriage, The: A Couple's Guide to Boosting Their Marriage Libido. Michele Weiner Davis. New York: Simon & Schuster, Inc., 2003.

What to do about inequality in marriage and in bed, when one partner has more sexual desire than the other, and/or has more desire to work on other aspects of the relationship.

Your Long Erotic Weekend: Four Days of Passion for a Lifetime of Magnificent Sex. Lana Holstein, M.D. and David Taylor, M.D. Gloucester, MA: Four Winds Press, 2004.

The authors, physicians who have been married (to each other) for twenty-eight years, offer step-by-step guidance on giving and receiving sexual pleasure in ways that will intensify and expand both partners' sexual horizons, based on the authors created their workshops at Canyon Ranch Health Spa (and now at Miraval Life in Balance Resort).

8. Share the Work and Decision Making

Life Matters: Creating a Dynamic Balance of Work, Family, Time and Money. A. Roger Merrill, Rebecca R. Merrill. New York: McGraw-Hill, 2003.

The Merrills, time management experts who coauthored *First Things First* with Stephen Covey, cover ways to successfully balance four major aspects of life: family, money, work, and time. They offer skills and inspiration to help you make the changes necessary to have internal peace and improved relationships.

The Second Shift. Arlie Hochschild and Anne Machung. New York: Penguin, 2003.

A thought-provoking, timeless report on reconciling economic and personal needs with having children. Relevant for couples who are deciding on careers, getting married, or already trying to balance both.

9. Enjoy Raising Children

Get Out of My Life: But First Could You Drive Me and Cheryl to the Mall? A Parent's Guide to the New Teenager. Anthony E. Wolf, Ph.D. New York: Farrar Straus Giroux, 1991.

A psychologist with years of experience counseling teens tells what parents can—and can't—do to help their kids through the unavoidable growing pains of adolescence. The author cautions that conflict is inevitable, but gives advice on avoiding unnecessary friction.

How to Negotiate with Kids Even When You Think You Shouldn't. Scott Brown. New York: Viking, Inc., 2003.

The author, a founder of the Harvard Negotiating Project, had the idea of bringing negotiating skills to bear on his four kids. He explains how to focus on the problem at hand, not the child, and how strategies must change as kids grow older.

How to Talk So Kids Will Listen and Listen So Kids Will Talk. 20th anniversary edition. Adele Faber, Elaine Mazlish. New York: Avon, 1999.

The author provides a step-by-step guide on how to improve relationships in your household, and above all, stop fighting with your kids. The "reminder" pages and exercises are useful, as are this edition's feedback from two decades of readership.

The 10 Basic Principles of Good Parenting. Laurence Steinberg. New York: Simon & Schuster, Inc., 2004.

A psychologist at Temple University summarizes the ways that good parenting doesn't change across lines of race and class, or even as households are being stressed by two-income careers and the isolating effects of technology. Principle No. 1: "What You Do Matters."

What to Expect in the First Year. 2nd ed. Heidi Murkoff, Sandee Hathaway, and Arlene Eisenberg. New York: Workman Publishing Company: 2003.

A modern baby-and-mother-care bible, in an accessible month-by-month format, that includes the most recent developments in pediatric medicine. *What to Expect in the Toddler Years* is the equally accessible and helpful guide to the active and challenging years of toddlerhood.

Your Baby and Child from Birth to Age Five. Penelope Leach. New York: Alfred A. Knopf, 1997.

Sensible advice on the basics from a doctor with wide experience on child rearing, including feeding, sleeping, crying, comforting, teaching, and loving your baby.

10. Build a Happy, Healthy Life Together

The Canyon Ranch Guide to Living Younger Longer: A Complete Program for Optimal Health for Body, Mind, and Spirit. The staff of Canyon Ranch. New York: Simon & Schuster, 2001.

An easy-to-follow guide to getting fit, strong, and healthy in a balanced way that you can follow for a lifetime. This book includes advice on emotional and sexual intimacy.

Eight Weeks to Optimum Health: A Proven Program for Taking Advantage of Your Body's Natural Healing Powers. Andrew Weil, M.D. New York: Ballantine Publishing Group, 1997.

Dr. Weil outlines a program that you can follow in eight weeks to get yourself on the road to health and healing, complete with anecdotes from patients, his own experience, and examples of customized plans depending on your age or circumstances.

Learned Optimism: How to Change Your Mind and Your Life. Martin E.P. Seligman, Ph.D. New York: Pocket Books, 1990.

Seligman, the author of *Authentic Happiness,* proposes that there are two ways of looking at the world and even the most confirmed pessimist can learn to see the world in a different and happier way. Even better, you can teach your children that optimistic view of the world, too.

Meditation for Beginners. Jack Kornfield. Boulder, CO: Sounds True, 2004.

Breathing, posture, attention, forgiveness—it's all explained for you, with a CD to boot.

Miracle of Mindfulness: An Introduction to the Practice of Meditation. Thich Nhat Hanh. Boston: Beacon Press, 1975.

This Zen master speaks in the first person, simply and directly, about how to learn the skills of mindfulness, to allow you to feel awake and aware in a busy world.

1,000 Places to See Before You Die. Patricia Schultz. New York: Workman Publishing Company, 2003.

A joyous, passionate, around-the-world, continent-by-continent listing of beaches, museums, monuments, islands, inns, restaurants, mountains, and more, both on and off the beaten path.

Peace Is Every Step: The Path of Mindfulness in Everyday Life. Thich Nhat Hanh. New York: Bantam, 1992.

The meditations Thich Nhat Hanh has been celebrated for worldwide are captured within this deceptively slim book. It is a remarkable starting point for anyone wanting to learn about Buddhism, searching for balance in their lives; it's also for non-Buddhists who are simply looking for a way to find peace and bridge the gap of divisiveness.

Reversing Heart Disease. Dr. Dean Ornish. New York: Ballantine Books, 1990.

Whether you actually suffer from cardiovascular problems or not, Dr. Ornish lets you know what you need to do in the way of eating, exercising, and changing your attitude in life to reduce stress and prevent—or even reverse—the harmful effects of heart disease.

Ten Fun Things to Do Before You Die. Karol Jackowski. New York: Hyperion Press, 2000.

The author is a nun who insists that the way to stop taking yourself overseriously is to wake up to the fact that life is basically enjoyable. Find something to laugh about. "Time rarely gets more divine than that."

Yoga for Wimps: Poses for the Flexibly Impaired. Miriam Austin. New York: Sterling Publishing, 1999.

Starts with "instant" sessions you can do at any time of day. The photographs of correct positions make it easy to learn.

About the Authors

LILO and GERARD LEEDS met in a ski lodge in the Adirondack Mountains in 1950, were married in 1951, and now, more than fifty years later, have a family of five children and thirteen grandchildren. They still ski together as a family as often as possible.

Together Lilo and Gerry launched a major high-tech publishing company, which grew over the next thirty years into a $500 million organization, with more than 1,500 employees, and became a leader in providing information and Internet services for the high-tech industries. The company's socially responsible policies—and especially its on-site day care center—helped it win countless awards for being a great place to work.

In 1990 they turned the management of the company over to two of their sons, Michael and Daniel, and, with the help of their son, Greg, devoted themselves to working on improving public education for children growing up in poverty. When the Leeds sold the company in 1999, they divided some of the profits among all their employees and founded several of their not-for-profit organizations that are dedicated to children at risk. All profits from this book will go to the education foundations.

Lilo and Gerry hold degrees in math and science, respectively, received their master's degrees together in liberal arts, and have, between them, seven honorary doctorates. They live on Long Island, New York.

TERRENCE REAL has been a family therapist and teacher for more than twenty years. The bestselling author of *I Don't Want to Talk About It: Overcoming the Secret Legacy of Male Depression* (Scribner, 1997), *How Can I Get Through to You? Reconnecting Men and Women* (Scribner, 2002), and *The New Rules of Marriage: What You Need to Know to Make Love Work*, Terry knows how to lead couples on a step-by-step journey to greater intimacy—and greater personal fulfillment.

A senior faculty member of the Family Institute of Cambridge in Massachusetts and a Clinical Fellow of the Meadows Institute in Arizona, Terry founded his own center, the Relational Life Institute, in March of 2002. Through his books, the Institute, and workshops around the country, Terry helps women and men break through outdated notions to find true connection and satisfaction.

Terry's work, with its rigorous common-sense approach, speaks to both men and women. His ideas on men's issues and on couples therapy have been celebrated in venues from the *Today Show* and *20/20*, to *Oprah* and *The New York Times*.

Terry lives with his wife, family therapist Belinda Berman, and their two sons in Newton, Massachusetts.

SUSAN SELIGER is an award-winning writer, magazine editor, editorial and marketing consultant, and professional storyteller. She is the author of *Stop Killing Yourself: Make Stress Work for You*; a chapter of that health book is currently on display as an interactive exhibit called, "How Old Are You *Really*?" in half a dozen science museums across the US and in Belfast, Ireland.

A former deputy editor of *Good Housekeeping* and *Working Mother Magazine* and deputy editor in magazine development at Hearst and a consulting editor in magazine development at Time Inc., Seliger has helped launch several national Web sites and her articles have appeared in dozens of leading publications, including *New York Magazine, Family Circle, Redbook, Travel & Leisure, USA Today, The Economist, The Washington Post, The Chicago Tribune,* and *The Miami Herald.*